Building iPhone Apps with HTML, CSS, and JavaScript

Building iPhone Apps with HTML, CSS, and JavaScript

Jonathan Stark

O'REILLY®

Beijing · Cambridge · Farnham · Köln · Sebastopol · Taipei · Tokyo

Building iPhone Apps with HTML, CSS, and JavaScript
by Jonathan Stark

Published by O'Reilly Media, Inc., 1005 Gravenstein Highway North, Sebastopol, CA 95472.

O'Reilly books may be purchased for educational, business, or sales promotional use. Online editions are also available for most titles (*http://my.safaribooksonline.com*). For more information, contact our corporate/institutional sales department: (800) 998-9938 or *corporate@oreilly.com*.

Editor: Brian Jepson	**Indexer:** Fred Brown
Production Editor: Sumita Mukherji	**Cover Designer:** Karen Montgomery
Copyeditor: Emily Quill	**Interior Designer:** David Futato
Proofreader: Sada Preisch	**Illustrator:** Robert Romano

Printing History:

January 2010:   First Edition.

RepKover.   This book uses RepKover™, a durable and flexible lay-flat binding.

ISBN: 978-0-596-80578-4

[M]

1262956714

*To Erica—and that little jumping bean in her
tummy.*

Table of Contents

Preface

Like millions of people, I fell in love with my iPhone immediately. Initially, web apps were the only way to get a custom app on the device, which was fine by me because I'm a web developer. Months later when the App Store was announced, I was jacked. I ran out and bought every Objective-C book on the market. Some of my web apps were already somewhat popular, and I figured I'd just rewrite them as native apps, put them in the App Store, and ride off into the sunset on a big, galloping pile of money.

Disillusionment followed. I found it difficult to learn Objective-C, and I was turned off by the fact that the language was of little use outside of Mac programming. Xcode and Interface Builder were pretty slick, but they weren't my normal authoring environment and I found them hard to get accustomed to. I was infuriated by the hoops I had to jump through just to set my app and iPhone for testing. The process of getting the app into the App Store was even more byzantine. After a week or two of struggling with these variables, I found myself wondering why I was going to all the trouble. After all, my web apps were already available worldwide—why did I care about being in the App Store?

On top of all this, Apple can—and does—reject apps. This is certainly their prerogative, and maybe they have good reasons. However, from the outside, it seems capricious and arbitrary. Put yourself in these shoes (based on a true story, BTW): you spend about 100 hours learning Objective-C. You spend another 100 hours or so writing a native iPhone app. Eventually, your app is ready for prime time and you successfully navigate the gauntlet that is the App Store submission process. What happens next?

You wait. And wait. And wait some more. We are talking weeks, and sometimes months. Finally you hear back! And...your app is rejected. Now what? You have nothing to show for your effort. The bubble.

But wait, it can get worse. Let's say you do get your app approved. Hundreds or maybe thousands of people download your app. You haven't received any money yet, but you are on cloud nine. Then, the bug reports start coming in. You locate and fix the bug in minutes, resubmit your app to iTunes, and wait for Apple to approve the revision. And wait. And wait some more. Angry customers are giving you horrible reviews in the App Store. Your sales are tanking. And still you wait. You consider offering a refund to the angry customers, but there's no way to do that through the App Store. So you are basically forced to sit there watching your ratings crash even though the bug was fixed days or weeks ago.

Sure, this story is based on the experience of one developer. Maybe it's an edge case and the actual data doesn't bear out my thesis. But the problem remains: we developers have no access to Apple's data, or the real details of the App Store approval process. Until that changes, building a native app with Objective-C is a risky proposition.

Fortunately, there is an alternative. You can build a web app using open source, standards-based web technologies, release it as a web app, and debug and test it under load with real users. Once you are ready to rock, you can use PhoneGap to convert your web app to a native iPhone app and submit it to the App Store. If it's ultimately rejected, you aren't dead in your tracks because you can still offer the web app. If it's approved, great! You can then start adding features that enhance your web app by taking advantage of the unique hardware features available on the device. Sounds like the best of both worlds, right?

Who Should Read This Book

I'm going to assume that you have some basic experience reading and writing HTML, CSS, and JavaScript (jQuery in particular). I will be including some basic SQL code in Chapters 5 and 6, so a passing familiarity with SQL syntax would be helpful but is not required.

What You Need to Use This Book

This book is going to avoid the iPhone SDK wherever possible. All you'll need to follow along with the vast majority of examples is a text editor and the most recent version of Safari (or better yet, WebKit, which is a more cutting-edge version of Safari that's available for both Mac and Windows at *http://webkit.org*). You do need a Mac for the PhoneGap material in Chapter 7, where I explain how to convert your web app into a native app that you can submit to the App Store.

Conventions Used in This Book

The following typographical conventions are used in this book:

Italic

    Indicates new terms, URLs, email addresses, filenames, and file extensions.

`Constant width`

    Used for program listings, as well as within paragraphs to refer to program elements such as variable or function names, databases, data types, environment variables, statements, and keywords.

Constant width bold

> Shows commands or other text that should be typed literally by the user and for emphasis within code listings.

Constant width italic

> Shows text that should be replaced with user-supplied values or by values determined by context.

 This icon signifies a tip, suggestion, or general note.

 This icon indicates a warning or caution.

Using Code Examples

This book is here to help you get your job done. In general, you may use the code in this book in your programs and documentation. You do not need to contact us for permission unless you're reproducing a significant portion of the code. For example, writing a program that uses several chunks of code from this book does not require permission. Selling or distributing a CD-ROM of examples from O'Reilly books does require permission. Answering a question by citing this book and quoting example code does not require permission. Incorporating a significant amount of example code from this book into your product's documentation does require permission.

We appreciate, but do not require, attribution. An attribution usually includes the title, author, publisher, and ISBN. For example: *"Building iPhone Apps with HTML, CSS, and JavaScript* by Jonathan Stark. Copyright 2010 Jonathan Stark, 978-0-596-80578-4."

If you feel your use of code examples falls outside fair use or the permission given above, feel free to contact us at *permissions@oreilly.com*.

Safari® Books Online

 Safari Books Online is an on-demand digital library that lets you easily search over 7,500 technology and creative reference books and videos to find the answers you need quickly.

With a subscription, you can read any page and watch any video from our library online. Read books on your cell phone and mobile devices. Access new titles before they are available for print, and get exclusive access to manuscripts in development and post feedback for the authors. Copy and paste code samples, organize your favorites, download chapters, bookmark key sections, create notes, print out pages, and benefit from tons of other time-saving features.

O'Reilly Media has uploaded this book to the Safari Books Online service. To have full digital access to this book and others on similar topics from O'Reilly and other publishers, sign up for free at *http://my.safaribooksonline.com*.

How to Contact Us

Please address comments and questions concerning this book to the publisher:

> O'Reilly Media, Inc.
> 1005 Gravenstein Highway North
> Sebastopol, CA 95472
> 800-998-9938 (in the United States or Canada)
> 707-829-0515 (international or local)
> 707-829-0104 (fax)

We have a web page for this book, where we list errata, examples, and any additional information. You can access this page at:

> *http://www.oreilly.com/catalog/9780596805784/*

To comment or ask technical questions about this book, send email to:

> *bookquestions@oreilly.com*

For more information about our books, conferences, Resource Centers, and the O'Reilly Network, see our website at:

> *http://www.oreilly.com*

Acknowledgments

Writing a book is a team effort. My heartfelt thanks go out to the following people for their generous contributions.

Tim O'Reilly, Brian Jepson, and the rest of the gang at ORM for making the experience of writing this book so rewarding and educational.

Jack Templin, Providence Geeks, and RI Nexus for introducing me to the thriving tech scene in my own hometown. This book wouldn't exist if it weren't for Providence Geeks.

David Kandeda for his wonderfully obsessive pursuit of beauty. Whether it's a bit of code, or a user interface animation, he can't sleep until it's perfect, and I love that.

Brian LeRoux, Brock Whitten, Rob Ellis, and the rest of the gang at Nitobi for creating and continuing to support PhoneGap.

Brian Fling for broadening my view of mobile beyond just the latest and greatest hardware. Brian knows mobile from back in the day; he's a wonderful writer, and on top of that, a very generous guy.

PPK, John Gruber, John Allsopp, and John Resig for their contributions to and support of the underlying technologies that made this book possible.

Garrett Murray, Brian LeRoux, and the swarm of folks who generously posted comments and questions on the OFPS site for this book. Your feedback was very helpful and much appreciated.

Kazu, Chuckie, Janice, Chris, and the rest of the gang at Haruki for being so accommodating while I endlessly typed away at the high top by the door.

My wonderful family, friends, and clients for being understanding and supportive while I was chained to the keyboard.

And finally, Erica. You make everything possible. I love you!

CHAPTER 1

Getting Started

Before we dive in and start building applications for the iPhone, I'd like to quickly establish the playing field. In this chapter, I'll define key terms, compare the pros and cons of the two most common development approaches, and present a crash course in the three core web technologies that are used in this book.

Web Apps Versus Native Apps

First, I'll define what I mean by "web app" and "native app" and consider the pros and cons of each.

What Is a Web App?

To me, a web app is basically a website that is specifically optimized for the iPhone. The site can be anything from a standard small-business brochure site to a mortgage calculator to a daily calorie tracker—the content is irrelevant. The defining characteristics of a web app are that the user interface is built with web-standard technologies, it is available at a URL (public, private, or behind a login), and it is optimized for the specifics of the iPhone. A web app is not installed on the phone, is not available in the iTunes App Store, and is not written with Objective-C.

What Is a Native App?

In contrast, native apps are installed on the iPhone, have access to the hardware (speakers, accelerometer, camera, etc.), and are written with Objective-C. The defining characteristic of a native app, however, is that it's available in the iTunes App Store—a feature that has captured the imagination of hordes of software entrepreneurs worldwide, myself included.

Pros and Cons

Different applications have different requirements. Some apps are a better fit with web technologies than others. Knowing the pros and cons of each approach will help you make the right decision about which path is appropriate for your situation.

Here are the pros of native app development:

- Millions of registered credit card owners are one click away.
- Xcode, Interface Builder, and the Cocoa Touch framework constitute a pretty sweet development environment.
- You can access all the cool hardware features of the device.

Here are the cons of native app development:

- You have to pay to become an Apple developer.
- You are at the mercy of the Apple approval process.
- You have to develop using Objective-C.
- You have to develop on a Mac.
- You can't release bug fixes in a timely fashion.
- The development cycle is slow, and the testing cycle is constrained by the App Store's limitations.

Here are the pros of web app development:

- Web developers can use their current authoring tools.
- You can use your current web design and development skills.
- You are not limited to developing on the Mac OS.
- Your app will run on any device that has a web browser.
- You can fix bugs in real time.
- The development cycle is fast.

Here are the cons of web app development:

- You cannot access the all cool hardware features of the phone.
- You have to roll your own payment system if you want to charge for the app.
- It can be difficult to achieve sophisticated UI effects.

Which Approach Is Right for You?

Here's where it gets exciting. The always-online nature of the iPhone creates an environment in which the lines between a web app and a native app get blurry. There are even some little-known features of the iPhone that allow you to take a web app offline if you want (see Chapter 6). What's more, several third-party projects—of which

PhoneGap is the most notable—are actively developing solutions that allow web developers to take a web app and package it as a native app for the iPhone and other mobile platforms.

For me, this is the perfect blend. I can write in my native language, release a product as a pure web app (for the iPhone and any other devices that have a modern browser) without going through Apple's approval process, and use the same codebase to create an enhanced native version that can access the device hardware and potentially be sold in the App Store. And if Apple rejects it? No big deal, because I still have my online version. I can keep working on the native version while customers use the web app.

Web Programming Crash Course

The three main technologies we are going to use to build web apps are HTML, CSS, and JavaScript. I'd like to quickly cover each to make sure we're all on the same page before plowing into the fancy stuff.

Intro to HTML

When you're browsing the Web, the pages that you are viewing are just text documents sitting on someone else's computer. The text in a typical web page is wrapped in HTML tags, which tell your browser about the structure of the document. With this information, the browser can decide how to display the information in a way that makes sense.

Consider the web page snippet shown in Example 1-1. On the first line, the string Hi there! is wrapped in a pair of h1 tags. (Notice that the open tag and the close tag are slightly different: the close tag has a slash as the second character, while the open tag does not.)

Wrapping some text in h1 tags tells the browser that the words enclosed are a heading, which will cause it to be displayed in large bold text on its own line. There are also h2, h3, h4, h5, and h6 heading tags. The lower the number, the more important the header, so text wrapped in an h6 tag will be smaller (i.e., less important-looking) than text wrapped in an h3 tag.

After the h1 tag in Example 1-1 are two lines wrapped in p tags. These are called paragraph tags. Browsers will display each paragraph on its own line. If the paragraph is long enough to exceed the width of the browser window, the text will bump down and continue on the next line. In either case, a blank line will be inserted after the paragraph to separate it from the next item on the page.

Example 1-1. HTML snippet

```
<h1>Hi there!</h1>
<p>Thanks for visiting my web page.</p>
<p>I hope you like it.</p>
```

You can also put HTML tags inside of other HTML tags. Example 1-2 shows an unordered list (ul) tag that contains three list items (li). In a browser, this would show up as a bulleted list, with each item on its own line. When you have a tag or tags inside of another tag, the inner tags are called child elements, or children, of the parent tag. So in this example, the lis are children of the ul parent.

Example 1-2. Unordered list

```
<ul>
    <li>Pizza</li>
    <li>Beer</li>
    <li>Dogs</li>
</ul>
```

The tags I've covered so far are all *block tags*. The defining characteristic of a block tag is that it is displayed on a line of its own, with no elements to its left or right. That is why headings, paragraphs, and list items progress down the page instead of across it. The opposite of a block tag is an *inline tag*, which, as the name implies, can appear in a line. The emphasis tag (em) is an example of an inline tag, and it looks like this:

```
<p>I <em>really</em> hope you like it.</p>
```

The granddaddy of the inline tags—and arguably the coolest feature of HTML—is the a tag. The a stands for anchor, but I'll also refer to the tag as a link or hyperlink. Text wrapped in an anchor tag becomes clickable, such that clicking on it causes your browser to load a new HTML page.

In order to tell the browser what new page to load, we have to add what's called an *attribute* to the tag. Attributes are named values that are inserted into an open tag. In an anchor tag, you use the href attribute to specify the location of the target page. Here's a link to Google's home page:

```
<a href="http://www.google.com/">Google</a>
```

That might look like a bit of a jumble if you are not used to reading HTML, but you should be able to pick out the URL for the Google home page. You'll be seeing a lot of a tags and hrefs throughout the book, so take a minute to get your head around this if it doesn't make sense at first glance.

 There are a couple of things to keep in mind regarding attributes. Different HTML tags allow different attributes. You can add multiple attributes to an open tag by separating them with spaces. You never add attributes to a closing tag. There are hundreds of possible combinations of attributes and tags, but don't sweat it. We only have to worry about a dozen or so in this book.

The HTML snippet that we've been looking at would normally reside in the **body** section of a complete HTML document. An HTML document is made up of two sections: the head and the body. The body is where you put all the content that you want users to see. The head contains information about the page, most of which is invisible to the user.

The body and head are always wrapped in an `html` element. Example 1-3 shows the snippet in the context of a proper HTML document. For now the `head` section contains a `title` element, which tells the browser what text to display in the title bar of the window.

Example 1-3. A proper HTML document

```html
<html>
    <head>
        <title>My Awesome Page</title>
    </head>
    <body>
        <h1>Hi there!</h1>
        <p>Thanks for visiting my web page.</p>
        <p>I hope you like it.</p>
        <ul>
            <li>Pizza</li>
            <li>Beer</li>
            <li>Dogs</li>
        </ul>
    </body>
</html>
```

Normally, when you are using your web browser you are viewing pages that are hosted on the Internet. However, browsers are perfectly good at displaying HTML documents that are on your local machine as well. To see what I mean, crack open a text editor and type up Example 1-3. When you are done, save it to your desktop as *test.html* and then open it with Safari by either dragging the file onto the Safari application icon or opening Safari and selecting File→Open File. Double-clicking *test.html* might work as well, but it could open in your text editor or another browser depending on your settings.

 Even if you aren't running Mac OS X, you should use Safari when testing your iPhone web apps on a desktop web browser, because Safari is the closest desktop browser to the iPhone's Mobile Safari. Safari for Windows is available from *http://www.apple.com/safari/*.

Some text editors are bad for authoring HTML. In particular, you want to avoid editors that support rich text editing, like Microsoft Word or TextEdit. These types of editors can save their files in formats other than plain text, which will break your HTML. If you are in the market for a good text editor, my favorite by far on the Mac is TextMate (*http:// macromates.com/*), and I hear that there is a clone version for Windows called E Text Editor (*http://www.e-texteditor.com/*). If free is your thing, you can download Text Wrangler for Mac (*http://www.barebones.com/ products/TextWrangler/*) or use the built-in Notepad on Windows.

Intro to CSS

As you've seen, browsers render certain HTML elements with distinct styles (headings are large and bold, paragraphs are followed by a blank line, etc.). These styles are very basic and are primarily intended to help the reader understand the structure and meaning of the document.

To go beyond this simple structure-based rendering, you can use Cascading Style Sheets (CSS). CSS is a stylesheet language that is used to define the visual presentation of an HTML document. You can use CSS to define simple things like the text color, size, and style (bold, italic, etc.), or complex things like page layout, gradients, opacity, and much more.

Example 1-4 shows a CSS rule that instructs the browser to display any text in the body element using the color red. In this example, body is the *selector* (what is affected by the rule) and the curly braces enclose the *declaration* (the rule itself). The declaration includes a set of *properties* and their *values*. In this example, color is the property, and red is the value of the property.

Example 1-4. A simple CSS rule

```
body { color: red; }
```

Property names are predefined in the CSS specification, which means that you can't just make them up. Each property expects an appropriate value, and there can be lots of appropriate values and value formats for a given property.

For example, you can specify colors with predefined keywords like red, or by using HTML color code notation. This uses a hexadecimal notation: three pairs of hexadecimal digits (0–F) representing (from left to right) Red, Green, and Blue values. Properties that expect measurements can accept values like 10px, 75%, and 1em. Example 1-5 shows some common declarations. (The color code shown for background-color corresponds to the CSS "gray".)

Example 1-5. Some common CSS declarations

```
body {
    color: red;
    background-color: #808080;
```

```
    font-size: 12px;
    font-style: italic;
    font-weight: bold;
    font-family: Arial;
}
```

Selectors come in a variety of flavors. If you wanted all of your hyperlinks (the a element) to display in italics, you would add the following to your stylesheet:

```
a { font-style: italic; }
```

If you wanted to be more specific and only italicize the hyperlinks that were contained somewhere within an h1 tag, you would add the following to your stylesheet:

```
h1 a { font-style: italic; }
```

You can also define your own custom selectors by adding id and/or class attributes to your HTML tags. Consider the following HTML snippet:

```
<h1 class="loud">Hi there!</h1>
<p id="highlight">Thanks for visiting my web page.</p>
<p>I hope you like it.</p>
<ul>
    <li class="loud">Pizza</li>
    <li>Beer</li>
    <li>Dogs</li>
</ul>
```

If I added .loud { font-style: italic; } to the CSS for this HTML, Hi there! and Pizza would show up italicized because they both have the loud class. The dot in front of the .loud selector is important. It's how the CSS knows to look for HTML tags with a class of loud. If you omit the dot, the CSS would look for a loud tag, which doesn't exist in this snippet (or in HTML at all, for that matter).

Applying CSS by id is similar. To add a yellow background fill to the highlight paragraph tag, you'd use this rule:

```
#highlight { background-color: yellow; }
```

Here, the # symbol tells the CSS to look for an HTML tag with the id highlight.

To recap, you can opt to select elements by tag name (e.g., body, h1, p), by class name (e.g., .loud, .subtle, .error), or by id (e.g., #highlight, #login, #promo). And you can get more specific by chaining selectors together (e.g., h1 a, body ul .loud).

 There are differences between class and id. class attributes should be used when you have more than one item on the page with the same class value. Conversely, id values have to be unique to a page.

When I first learned this, I figured I'd just always use class attributes so I wouldn't have to worry about whether I was duping an id value. However, selecting elements by id is much faster than selecting them by class, so you can hurt your performance by overusing class selectors.

So now you understand the basics of CSS. But how do you apply a style sheet to an HTML page? It's actually quite simple. You just link to the stylesheet in the head of the HTML document, as seen in Example 1-6. The `href` attribute in this example is a relative path, meaning that it points to a text file named *screen.css* in the same directory as the HTML page. You can also specify absolute links, such as:

```
http://example.com/screen.css
```

Example 1-6. Linking to a CSS stylesheet

```html
<html>
    <head>
        <title>My Awesome Page</title>
        <link rel="stylesheet" href="screen.css" type="text/css" />
    </head>
    <body>
        <h1 class="loud">Hi there!</h1>
        <p id="highlight">Thanks for visiting my web page.</p>
        <p>I hope you like it.</p>
        <ul>
            <li class="loud">Pizza</li>
            <li>Beer</li>
            <li>Dogs</li>
        </ul>
    </body>
</html>
```

Example 1-7 shows the contents of *screen.css*. You should save this file in the same location as the HTML file.

Example 1-7. A simple stylesheet

```css
body {
    font-size: 12px;
    font-weight: bold;
    font-family: Arial;
}

a { font-style: italic; }
h1 a { font-style: italic; }

.loud { font-style: italic; }
#highlight { background-color: yellow; }
```

 It's worth pointing out that it's possible to link to stylesheets that are hosted on domains other than the one hosting the HTML document. However, it's considered very rude to link to someone else's stylesheets without permission, so please only link to your own.

For a quick and thorough crash course in CSS, I highly recommend *CSS Pocket Reference* by Eric Meyer (O'Reilly). Eric has the last word when it comes to CSS, and this particular book is short enough to read during the typical morning carpool. Unless you are the person driving, in which case it could take considerably longer (did I say "crash" course?).

Intro to JavaScript

At this point you should know how to structure a document with HTML, and how to modify its visual presentation with CSS. Now we'll add some JavaScript to make it do stuff.

JavaScript is a scripting language that can be added to an HTML page to make it more interactive and convenient for the user. For example, you can write some JavaScript that will inspect the values typed in a form to make sure they are valid. Or you can have JavaScript show or hide elements of a page depending on where the user clicks. JavaScript can even contact the web server to execute database changes without refreshing the current web page.

Like any modern scripting language, JavaScript has variables, arrays, objects, and all the typical control structures (if, while, for, and so on). Example 1-8 shows a snippet of JavaScript that illustrates several core concepts of the language.

Example 1-8. Basic JavaScript syntax

```
var foods = ['Apples', 'Bananas', 'Oranges']; ❶
for (var i in foods) { ❷
  if (foods[i] == 'Apples') { ❸
    alert(foods[i] + ' are my favorite!'); ❹
  } else {
    alert(foods[i] + ' are okay.'); ❺
  }
}
```

Here's an explanation of what's happening here:

❶ Define an array named foods that contains three elements.

❷ Open a for loop that defines a variable named i that will contain the index of each element of the array during the loop.

❸ A garden-variety if checks to see if the current element of the array is equal to Apples.

❹ This is displayed if the current element of the array is equal to Apples.

❺ This is displayed if the current element of the array is *not* equal to Apples.

Here are some points about JavaScript's syntax that are worth noting:

- Statements are terminated with semicolons.
- Code blocks are enclosed in curly braces.
- Variables are declared using the **var** keyword.
- Array elements can be accessed with square bracket notation.

- Array keys are assigned beginning at 0.
- The single equals sign is the assignment operator.
- The double equals sign is the equivalence logical operator.
- The plus sign is the string concatenation operator.

For our purposes, the most important feature of JavaScript is that it can interact with the elements of an HTML page (the cool kids call this "manipulating the DOM"). Example 1-9 shows a simple bit of JavaScript that changes some text on the page when the user clicks on the h1.

 DOM stands for Document Object Model, and in this context it represents the browser's understanding of an HTML page. You can read more about the Document Object Model here: *http://en.wikipedia.org/wiki/Document_Object_Model*.

Example 1-9. Simple OnClick handler

```
<html>
    <head>
        <title>My Awesome Page</title>
        <script type="text/javascript" charset="utf-8"> ❶
            function sayHello() { ❷
                document.getElementById('foo').innerHTML = 'Hi there!'; ❸
            } ❹
        </script> ❺
    </head>
    <body>
        <h1 id="foo" onclick❻="sayHello()">Click me!</h1>
    </body>
</html>
```

Here's an explanation:

❶ I've added a script block to the head of the HTML document.

❷ Inside the script block, I've defined a single JavaScript function named sayHello().

❸ The sayHello() function contains a single statement, which tells the browser to "look through the document for an element that has the id 'foo', and set its innerHTML contents to 'Hi there!.'" The effect of this in the browser is that the text "Click me!" will be replaced with "Hi there!" when the user clicks on the h1 element.

❹ End of the sayHello() function.

❺ End of the script block.

❻ The onclick attribute of the h1 element tells the browser to do something when the user clicks on the h1, namely, to run the sayHello() function.

Back in the bad old days of web development, different browsers had different support for JavaScript. This meant that your code might run in Safari 2 but not in Internet Explorer 6. You had to take great pains to test each browser (and even different versions of the same browser) in order to make sure your code would work for everyone. As the number of browsers and browser versions grew, it became impossible to test and maintain your JavaScript code for every environment. At that time, web programming with JavaScript was hell.

Enter jQuery. jQuery is a relatively small JavaScript library that allows you to write your JavaScript code in a way that will work the same in a wide variety of browsers. What's more, it greatly simplifies a number of common web development tasks. For these reasons, I use jQuery in most of my web development work, and I'll be using it for the JavaScript examples in this book. Example 1-10 is a jQuery rewrite of Example 1-9.

Example 1-10. jQuery OnClick handler

```html
<html>
    <head>
        <title>My Awesome Page</title>
        <script type="text/javascript" src="jquery.js"></script> ❶
        <script type="text/javascript" charset="utf-8">
            function sayHello() {
                $('#foo').text('Hi there!'); ❷
            }
        </script>
    </head>
    <body>
        <h1 id="foo" onclick="sayHello()">Click me!</h1>
    </body>
</html>
```

❶ Here, I include the *jquery.js* library. I've used a relative path, meaning that the file exists in the same directory as the page that is using it, but I could have included it directly from a variety of places where it's available.

❷ Notice the reduction in the amount of code we need to write to replace the text in the h1 element. This might not seem like a big deal in such a trivial example, but I can assure you that it's a lifesaver in complex solutions.

We'll be seeing plenty of real-world jQuery examples later on, so I'm going to leave it at that for the moment.

jQuery downloads, documentation, and tutorials are available at *http://jquery.com*. To use jQuery, you will need to download it from the website, rename the file you downloaded (such as *jquery-1.3.2.min.js*) to *jquery.js*, and put a copy of it in the same directory as your HTML document.

CHAPTER 2

Basic iPhone Styling

Ultimately, we are going to build a native iPhone app using HTML, CSS, and JavaScript. The first step on this journey is to get comfortable styling HTML to look like an iPhone app. In this chapter, I'll show you how to apply CSS styles to a bunch of existing HTML pages so that they are easily navigable on an iPhone. So, in addition to moving closer to building a native app, you'll be learning a practical (and valuable) skill that you can use immediately.

Don't Have a Website?

If you've been testing all your web pages locally on your personal computer, you won't be able to view them on your iPhone without setting up a server. You have a few choices:

- Host your web pages on a web server (your Internet Service Provider likely offers a complimentary web hosting service) and connect to that server from your iPhone.

- Host your web pages on a web server running on your computer, and connect to that web server from your iPhone. This only works when your iPhone and your computer are on the same WiFi network.

- If you don't have an iPhone, you can simulate one using Safari. In Safari's advanced preferences, enable the Develop menu, then select Develop→User Agent and choose the version of Mobile Safari you want to simulate.

This chapter is set up so that you can try the examples as you read through it. So no matter which option you choose for viewing the web pages, try reloading them in a browser (preferably the iPhone browser) each time you add something new, and save one of the sample files.

First Steps

Theory is great, but I'm a "show me, don't tell me" kinda guy. So let's dive in.

Imagine that you have a website that you want to iPhone-ize (Figure 2-1). In this scenario, there are a number of easy things you can do to optimize a site for the iPhone. I'll go over your options in this chapter.

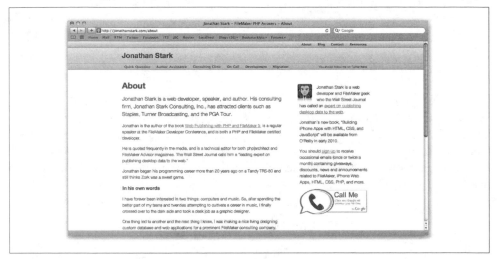

Figure 2-1. The desktop version of a typical web page looks fine in Safari on a computer

Figure 2-2 shows what the same web page looks like on the iPhone. It's usable, but far from optimized for the iPhone.

Figure 2-2. The same web page looks OK on an iPhone, but we can do much better

Example 2-1 shows an abbreviated version of the HTML for the web page shown in Figure 2-1. This is the HTML you'll be working with in this chapter. You can download it from the book's website (see "How to Contact Us" on page xiv) if you'd like to try styling it as you go through the chapter. The desktop stylesheet (*screen.css*) is not shown, as it is not essential, but you can use the stylesheet from the previous chapter if you'd like to have something to play with.

Example 2-1. The HTML document we'll be styling

```
<html>
<head>
  <link rel="stylesheet" href="screen.css" type="text/css" />
  <title>Jonathan Stark</title>
</head>
<body>
<div id="container">
  <div id="header">
    <h1><a href="./">Jonathan Stark</a></h1>
    <div id="utility">
        <ul>
            <li><a href="about.html">About</a></li>
            <li><a href="blog.html">Blog</a></li>
        </ul>
    </div>
    <div id="nav">
        <ul>
            <li><a href="consulting-clinic.html">Consulting Clinic</a></li>
            <li><a href="on-call.html">On Call</a></li>
            <li><a href="development.html">Development</a></li>
        </ul>
    </div>
  </div>
  <div id="content">
    <h2>About</h2>
    <p>Jonathan Stark is a web developer, speaker, and author. His
       consulting firm, Jonathan Stark Consulting, Inc., has attracted
       clients such as Staples, Turner Broadcasting, and the PGA Tour.
       ...
       </p>
  </div>
  <div id="sidebar">
    <img alt="Manga Portrait of Jonathan Stark"
        src="images/manga.png"
    <p>Jonathan Stark is a mobile and web application developer who the
       Wall Street Journal has called an expert on publishing desktop
       data to the web.</p>
  </div>
  <div id="footer">
    <ul>
        <li><a href="services.html">Services</a></li>
        <li><a href="about.html">About</a></li>
        <li><a href="blog.html">Blog</a></li>
    </ul>
    <p class="subtle">Jonathan Stark Consulting, Inc.</p>
```

```
    </div>
    </div>
    </body>
    </html>
```

 For years, web developers used tables to lay out elements in a grid. Advances in CSS and HTML have rendered that approach not only obsolete, but undesirable. Today, we primarily use the `div` element (along with a variety of attributes) to accomplish the same thing, but with more control. Although a complete explanation of `div`-based layouts is well beyond the scope of this book, you'll see plenty of examples of it as you read through the chapters. To learn more, check out *Designing with Web Standards* by Jeffrey Zeldman (New Riders Press), which covers the issue in greater detail.

Preparing a Separate iPhone Stylesheet

I'm as DRY as the next guy, but in the real world you're better off making a clean break between your desktop browser stylesheet and your iPhone stylesheet. Take my word for it and make two completely independent files—you'll sleep better. The alternative would be to wedge all of your CSS rules into a single stylesheet, which ends up being a bad idea for a number of reasons; the most obvious is that you'd be sending a bunch of irrelevant desktop style rules to the phone, which is a waste of precious bandwidth and memory.

 DRY stands for "Don't Repeat Yourself," and is a software development principle stating that "Every piece of knowledge must have a single, unambiguous, authoritative representation within a system." The term was coined by Andrew Hunt and David Thomas in their book *The Pragmatic Programmer* (Addison-Wesley).

To specify a stylesheet for the iPhone, replace the stylesheet link tag in the sample HTML document with ones that use the following expressions:

```
<link rel="stylesheet" type="text/css"
    href="iphone.css" media="only screen and (max-width: 480px)" />
<link rel="stylesheet" type="text/css"
    href="desktop.css" media="screen and (min-width: 481px)" />
```

Here, *desktop.css* refers to whatever your existing desktop stylesheet is, and *iphone.css* is a new file that we'll be discussing in detail in a bit.

If you're following along using the sample HTML document shown earlier, you'll now need to rename *screen.css* to *desktop.css*; however, since we're focused on the iPhone stylesheet, you can ignore the desktop stylesheet completely. If it fails to load, your browser won't get too upset.

Regrettably, Internet Explorer will not understand the previous expressions, so we have to add a conditional comment (shown in bold) that links to an IE-specific version of the CSS:

```
<link rel="stylesheet" type="text/css"
      href="iphone.css" media="only screen and (max-width: 480px)" />
<link rel="stylesheet" type="text/css"
      href="desktop.css" media="screen and (min-width: 481px)" />
<!--[if IE]>
<link rel="stylesheet" type="text/css" href="explorer.css" media="all" />
<![endif]-->
```

So now it's time to edit the HTML document: delete the existing link to the *screen.css* file and replace it with the lines just shown. This way, you will have a clean slate for the iPhone-specific CSS that I'll show you in this chapter.

Controlling the Page Scaling

Unless you tell it otherwise, Safari on the iPhone is going to assume that your page is 980px wide (Figure 2-3). In the majority of cases, this works great. However, you are going to format our content specifically for the smaller dimensions of the iPhone, so you must let Mobile Safari know about it by adding a viewport meta tag to the head element of the HTML document:

```
<meta name="viewport" content="user-scalable=no, width=device-width" />
```

If you don't set the viewport width, the page will be zoomed way out when it first loads.

The viewport meta tag will be ignored by browsers other than Mobile Safari, so you can include it without worrying about the desktop version of your site.

Merely by suppressing the desktop stylesheet and configuring your viewport, you are already giving your iPhone users an enhanced experience (Figure 2-4). To really impress them, let's start building the *iphone.css* stylesheet.

Figure 2-3. The iPhone assumes a normal web page is 980px wide

Figure 2-4. Setting the viewport to the width of the device makes your pages a lot more readable

Adding the iPhone CSS

There are a number of user interface (UI) conventions that make an iPhone app look like an iPhone app. In the next section, I'll add the distinctive title bar, lists with rounded corners, finger-friendly links that look like glossy buttons, and so on. Using your text editor, create a file named *iphone.css*, add the code in Example 2-2, and save the file in the same directory as your HTML document.

Example 2-2. Setting some general site-wide styles on the HTML body element

```
body {
    background-color: #ddd; /* Background color */
    color: #222;            /* Foreground color used for text */
    font-family: Helvetica;
    font-size: 14px;
    margin: 0;              /* Amount of negative space around the outside of the body */
    padding: 0;             /* Amount of negative space around the inside of the body */
}
```

> Note that I have set the overall font for the document to Helvetica, which is the font used by most of the applications on the iPhone. If you are trying to achieve a professional look, you should probably stick with Helvetica unless you have a specific reason not to.

Now I'll attack the header `div` that contains the main home link (i.e., the logo link) and the primary and secondary site navigation. The first step is to format the logo link as a clickable title bar. Add the following to the *iphone.css* file:

```
#header h1 {
    margin: 0;
    padding: 0;
}
#header h1 a {
    background-color: #ccc;
    border-bottom: 1px solid #666;
    color: #222;
    display: block;
    font-size: 20px;
    font-weight: bold;
    padding: 10px 0;
    text-align: center;
    text-decoration: none;
}
```

I'm going to format the primary and secondary navigation ul blocks identically, so I can just use the generic tag selectors (i.e., #header ul) as opposed to the tag ids (i.e., #header ul#utility, #header ul#nav):

```
#header ul {
    list-style: none;
    margin: 10px;
    padding: 0;
}
#header ul li a {
    background-color: #FFFFFF;
    border: 1px solid #999999;
    color: #222222;
    display: block;
    font-size: 17px;
    font-weight: bold;
    margin-bottom: -1px;
    padding: 12px 10px;
    text-decoration: none;
}
```

Pretty simple so far, right? With this little bit of CSS, we have already made a big improvement on the iPhone page design (Figure 2-5). Next, add some padding to the content and sidebar divs to indent the text from the edge of the screen a bit (Figure 2-6):

```
#content, #sidebar {
    padding: 10px;
}
```

Figure 2-5. A little bit of CSS can go a long way toward enhancing the usability of your iPhone app

Figure 2-6. Indenting text from the edges

You might be wondering why I added padding to the content and sidebar elements instead of setting it globally on the body element itself. The reason is that it's very common to have elements that you want to have displayed edge to edge (as with the header in this example). Because of this, padding applied to the body or some other global wrapper element can become more trouble than it's worth.

The content in the footer of this page is basically a rehash of the navigation element at the top of the page (the ul element with the id nav), so you can remove the footer from the iPhone version of the page by setting the display to none:

```
#footer {
    display: none;
}
```

Adding the iPhone Look and Feel

Now it's time to get a little fancier. Starting from the top of the page, add a 1-pixel white drop shadow to the logo link text, and a CSS gradient to the background:

```
#header h1 a {
    text-shadow: 0px 1px 0px #fff;
    background-image: -webkit-gradient(linear, left top, left bottom,
                                       from(#ccc), to(#999));
}
```

In the text-shadow declaration, the parameters from left to right are horizontal offset, vertical offset, blur, and color. Most of the time, you'll be applying the exact values shown here to your text because that's what usually looks good on the iPhone, but it is fun to experiment with `text-shadow` because it can add a subtle but sophisticated touch to your design.

The `-webkit-gradient` line deserves special attention. It's an instruction to the browser to generate a gradient image on the fly. Therefore, a CSS gradient can be used anywhere you would normally specify a `url()` (e.g., background image, list style image). The parameters from left to right are as follows: the gradient type (can be linear or radial), the starting point of the gradient (can be left top, left bottom, right top, or right bottom), the end point of the gradient, the starting color, and the ending color.

 Note that you cannot reverse the horizontal and vertical portions of the four gradient start and stop point constants (i.e., left top, left bottom, right top, and right bottom). In other words, top left, bottom left, top right, and bottom right are invalid values.

The next step is to add the traditional rounded corners to the navigation menus:

```
#header ul li:first-child a {
    -webkit-border-top-left-radius: 8px;
    -webkit-border-top-right-radius: 8px;
}
#header ul li:last-child a {
    -webkit-border-bottom-left-radius: 8px;
    -webkit-border-bottom-right-radius: 8px;
}
```

As you can see, I'm using corner-specific versions of the `-webkit-border-radius` property to apply an 8-pixel radius to both the top two corners of the first list item, and the bottom two corners of the last list item (Figure 2-7).

Figure 2-7. Gradients, text shadows, and rounded corners start to transform your web page into a native-looking iPhone app

It would be cool if you could just apply the border radius to the enclosing ul, but it doesn't work. If you try it, you'll see that the square corners of the child list items will overflow the rounded corners of the ul, thereby negating the effect.

 Technically, I could achieve the rounded list effect by applying the radius corners to the ul if I set the background color of the ul to white and the background of its child elements to transparent. However, when you click the first or last item in the list, the tap highlight will show up squared off and it looks terrible. Your best bet is to apply the rounding to the tags themselves as I've demonstrated here.

Adding Basic Behavior with jQuery

One of my favorite things about building web apps for the iPhone is that I can be reasonably sure that JavaScript is enabled. Regrettably, this is not the situation when building websites for desktop browsers. My next step is to add some JavaScript to my page to support some basic dynamic behavior. In particular, I want to allow users to show and hide the big honking navigation section in the header so that they only see it when they want to. In order to make this work, I'm going to write some new CSS, and use some JavaScript to apply the new CSS to the existing HTML.

First, let's take a look at the new CSS. Step one is to hide the ul elements in the header so they don't show up when the user first loads the page. If you are following along at home, open your *iphone.css* file and add the following:

```
#header ul.hide {
    display: none;
}
```

Next, I'll define the styles for the button that will show and hide the menu. Note that the button does not exist in the HTML yet; for your information, the HTML for the button is going to look like this:

```
<div class="leftButton" onclick="toggleMenu()">Menu</div>
```

I'll describe the button HTML in detail in a moment ("Adding Basic Behavior with jQuery" on page 25), so don't bother adding the preceding line of code to your HTML file yet. The important thing to note is that it's a div with the class leftButton and it's going to be in the header.

Here is the CSS style for the button (you can go ahead and add this to the *iphone.css* file):

```
#header div.leftButton {
    position: absolute;❶
    top: 7px;
    left: 6px;
    height: 30px;❷
    font-weight: bold;❸
    text-align: center;
    color: white;
```

```
        text-shadow: rgba(0,0,0,0.6) 0px -1px 0px;❹
        line-height: 28px;❺
        border-width: 0 8px 0 8px;❻
        -webkit-border-image: url(images/button.png) 0 8 0 8;❼
    }
```

 For the graphics used in this chapter, you can download jQTouch from *http://jqtouch.com/* and copy the graphics from the *themes/jqt/img* directory. Put these copies into an *images* subdirectory beneath the directory that contains your HTML document (you'll probably need to create the *images* directory). We'll be talking about jQTouch in detail in Chapter 4.

❶ Taking it from the top, I set the position to absolute to remove the `div` from the document flow, which allows me to set its top and left pixel coordinates.

❷ Here, I set the height to 30px so it's big enough to tap easily.

❸ Next, I style the text bold, white with a slight drop shadow, and centered in the box.

❹ In CSS, the `rgb` function is an alternative to the familiar hex notation typically used to specify colors (e.g., #FFFFFF). `rgb(255, 255, 255)` and `rgb(100%, 100%, 100%)` are both the same as #FFFFFF. More recently, the `rgba()` function has been introduced, which allows you to specify a fourth parameter that defines the alpha value (i.e., opacity) of the color. The range of allowable values is 0 to 1, where 0 is fully transparent and 1 is fully opaque; decimal values between 0 and 1 will be rendered translucent.

❺ The `line-height` declaration moves the text down vertically in the box so it's not flush up against the top border.

❻ The `border-width` and `-webkit-border-image` lines require a bit of explanation. These two properties together allow you to assign portions of a single image to the border area of an element. This means no more nonsemantic nested `div`s or slicing images into *topLeftCorner.png*, *topRightCorner.png*, etc. If the box resizes because the text increases or decreases, the border image will stretch to accommodate it. It's really a great thing; having fewer images means less work, less bandwidth, and shorter load times.

With the `border-width` line, I'm telling the browser to apply a 0 border to the top, an 8px border to the right, a 0-width border to the bottom, and an 8px-width border to the left (i.e., the four parameters start at the top of the box and work their way around clockwise). Note that I don't need to specify a color or style for the border.

❼ With the border widths in place, I can apply the border image. The five parameters from left to right are the `url` of the image, the top width, the right width, the bottom width, and the left width (again, clockwise from top). The url can be absolute (*http://*

example.com/myBorderImage.png) or relative. Relative paths are based on the location of the stylesheet, not the HTML page that includes the stylesheet.

When I first encountered the border image property, I found it odd that I had to specify the border widths when I had already done so with the border-width property. After some painful trial and error, I discovered that the widths in the border-image property are not border widths; they are the widths *to slice* from the image. Taking the right border as an example, I'm telling the browser to take the left 8 pixels of the image and apply them to the right border, which also happens to have an 8px width.

It is possible to do something irrational, such as applying the right 4 pixels of an image to a border that is 20px wide. To make this work properly, you have to use the optional parameters of webkit-border-image that tell the image what to do with the slice in the available border space (repeat, stretch, round, etc.). In three years of trying, I have failed to come up with any sane reason to do this, so I won't waste space here describing this confusing and impractical option of an otherwise killer feature.

OK, time for some JavaScript. In preparation for the JavaScript you're about to write, you need to update your HTML document to include *jquery.js* and *iphone.js*. Add these lines to the head section of your HTML document:

```
<script type="text/javascript" src="jquery.js"></script>
<script type="text/javascript" src="iphone.js"></script>
```

jQuery downloads, documentation, and tutorials are available at *http://jquery.com*. To use jQuery, you will need to download it from the website, rename the file you downloaded (such as *jquery-1.3.2.min.js*) to *jquery.js*, and put a copy of it in the same directory as your HTML document.

The primary duty of the JavaScript we need to write is to allow the user to show and hide the navigation menus. Copy the following JavaScript into a file called *iphone.js* and save it in the same folder as the HTML file:

```
if (window.innerWidth && window.innerWidth <= 480) { ❶
    $(document).ready(function(){ ❷
        $('#header ul').addClass('hide'); ❸
        $('#header').append('<div class="leftButton"
            onclick="toggleMenu()">Menu</div>'); ❹
    });
    function toggleMenu() {
        $('#header ul').toggleClass('hide'); ❺
        $('#header .leftButton').toggleClass('pressed'); ❻
    }
}
```

❶ The entire page is wrapped in an `if` statement that checks to make sure the `innerWidth` property of the `window` object exists (it doesn't exist in some versions of Internet Explorer) and that the width is less than or equal to 480 (the max width for the iPhone). By adding this line, we ensure that the code only executes when the user is browsing the page with an iPhone or some other similarly sized device.

 If you are testing your iPhone web pages using the desktop version of Safari as described in "Don't Have a Website?" on page 13, the `if` statement here will fail if your browser's window width is too large. As a workaround, enter the following line of JavaScript into Safari's location bar to resize your browser to more iPhone-esque dimensions:

`javascript:window.scrollTo(0,0);resizeTo(320,480);`

You can even increase the height measurement to make a tall skinny view which is sometimes helpful if you are working with a lot of content (Figure 2-10, shown later).

❷ Here we have the so-called "document ready" function. If you are new to jQuery, this can be a bit intimidating, and I admit that it took me a while to memorize the syntax. However, it's worth taking the time to commit it to memory because you'll be using it a lot. The document ready function basically says, "When the document is ready, run this code." More on why this is important in a sec.

❸ This is typical jQuery code that begins by selecting the `ul`s in the header and adding the "hide" CSS class to them. Remember, `hide` is the selector we used in the previous CSS. The net effect of executing this line is to "hide" the header `ul` elements. Take special note: had we not wrapped this line in the document ready function, it would have most likely executed before the `ul`s were even finished loading. This means that the JavaScript would load, this line would fail because the `ul`s wouldn't exist yet, the page would continue loading, the `ul`s would appear, and you'd be scratching your head (or smashing your keyboard) wondering why the JavaScript wasn't working.

❹ Here is where I append a button to the header that will allow the user to show and hide the menu (Figure 2-8). It has a class that corresponds to the CSS we wrote previously for `.leftButton`, and it has an `onclick` handler that calls the function `toggleMenu()`, which comes next.

❺ The `toggleMenu()` function uses jQuery's `toggleClass()` function to add or remove the specified class to the selected object. On this line, I'm toggling the `hide` class on the header `ul`s.

❻ Here, I'm toggling the `pressed` class on the header `leftButton`.

Figure 2-8. The Menu button has been added to the toolbar dynamically using jQuery

We haven't written the CSS for the `pressed` class yet, so let's do so now. Go back to *iphone.css* and insert the following:

```
#header div.pressed {
    -webkit-border-image: url(images/button_clicked.png) 0 8 0 8;
}
```

As you can see, I'm simply specifying a different image for the button border (it happens to be slightly darker). This will add a two-state effect to the button that should make it evident to the user that the button can both show and hide the menu (Figure 2-9).

Figure 2-9. The Menu button displays darker when it has been pressed to display the menu options

Figure 2-10. A tall view of the completed basic iPhone CSS

What You've Learned

In this chapter, I covered the basics of converting an existing web page to a more iPhone-friendly format. I even used a bit of dynamic HTML to show and hide the navigation panels. In the next chapter, I'll build on these examples while introducing some more advanced JavaScript concepts—in particular, some yummy Ajax goodness.

CHAPTER 3

Advanced iPhone Styling

In our quest to build an iPhone app without Objective-C, we've so far learned how to use CSS to style a collection of HTML pages to *look* like an iPhone app. In this chapter, we'll lay the groundwork to make those same pages *behave* like an iPhone app. Specifically, we'll discuss using Ajax to turn a full website into a single-page app, how to create a back button with history using JavaScript, and how to take advantage of the Web Clip icon and full screen mode features of the iPhone to launch your app without Mobile Safari intruding upon the user experience.

Adding a Touch of Ajax

The term Ajax has become such a buzzword that I'm not even sure I know what it means anymore. For the purposes of this book, I'm going to use Ajax to refer to the technique of using JavaScript to send requests to a web server without reloading the current page (e.g., to retrieve some HTML, submit a form, and so on). This approach makes for a very smooth user experience, but does require that you reinvent a lot of wheels.

For example, if you are loading external pages dynamically, the browser will not give any indication of progress or errors to the users. Furthermore, the back button will not work as expected unless you take pains to support it. In other words, you have to do a lot of work to make a sweet Ajax app. Even so, there are some very good reasons to go to the trouble. In particular, it opens the door to creating iPhone apps that can run full-screen ("Full Screen Mode" on page 48) and even offline (Chapter 6).

Traffic Cop

For my next series of examples, I'm going to write a single page called *iphone.html* that will sit in front of all of the site's other pages and will handle requests, sort of like a traffic cop. Here's how it works. On first load, *iphone.html* will present the user with a nicely formatted version of the site navigation. I'll then use jQuery to "hijack" the onclick actions of the nav links so that when the user clicks on one, the browser page will *not* navigate to the target link. Rather, jQuery will load a portion of the HTML from the remote page and deliver the data to the user by updating the current page. I'll start with the most basic functional version of the code and improve it as we go along.

The HTML for the *iphone.html* wrapper page is extremely simple (see Example 3-1). In the head section, I set the title and viewport options, and include links to a stylesheet (*iphone.css*) and two JavaScript files: *jquery.js* and a custom JavaScript file named *iphone.js*.

 For more information on where to get *jquery.js* and what to do with it, see "Intro to JavaScript" on page 9.

The body just has two div containers: a header with the initial title in an h1 tag, and an empty div container, which will end up holding HTML snippets retrieved from other pages.

Example 3-1. This simple HTML wrapper markup will sit in front of all the site's other pages

```
<html>
<head>
    <title>Jonathan Stark</title>
    <meta name="viewport" content="user-scalable=no, width=device-width" />
    <link rel="stylesheet" href="iphone.css" type="text/css" media="screen" />
    <script type="text/javascript" src="jquery.js"></script>
    <script type="text/javascript" src="iphone.js"></script>
</head>
<body>
    <div id="header"><h1>Jonathan Stark</h1></div>
    <div id="container"></div>
</body>
</html>
```

Moving on to the *iphone.css* file, you can see in Example 3-2 that I've reshuffled some of the properties from previous examples (e.g., some of the #header h1 properties have been moved up to #header). Overall, though, everything should look familiar (if not, please review Chapter 2).

Example 3-2. The base CSS for the page is just a slightly reshuffled version of previous examples

```
body {
    background-color: #ddd;
    color: #222;
    font-family: Helvetica;
    font-size: 14px;
    margin: 0;
    padding: 0;
}
#header {
```

```css
    background-color: #ccc;
    background-image: -webkit-gradient(linear, left top, left bottom, from(#ccc), to(#999));
    border-color: #666;
    border-style: solid;
    border-width: 0 0 1px 0;
}
#header h1 {
    color: #222;
    font-size: 20px;
    font-weight: bold;
    margin: 0 auto;
    padding: 10px 0;
    text-align: center;
    text-shadow: 0px 1px 0px #fff;
}
ul {
    list-style: none;
    margin: 10px;
    padding: 0;
}
ul li a {
    background-color: #FFF;
    border: 1px solid #999;
    color: #222;
    display: block;
    font-size: 17px;
    font-weight: bold;
    margin-bottom: -1px;
    padding: 12px 10px;
    text-decoration: none;
}
ul li:first-child a {
    -webkit-border-top-left-radius: 8px;
    -webkit-border-top-right-radius: 8px;
}
ul li:last-child a {
    -webkit-border-bottom-left-radius: 8px;
    -webkit-border-bottom-right-radius: 8px;
}
ul li a:active,ul li a:hover {
    background-color:blue;
    color:white;
}
#content {
    padding: 10px;
    text-shadow: 0px 1px 0px #fff;
}
#content a {
    color: blue;
}
```

The JavaScript in *iphone.js* is where all the magic happens in this example. Please refer to Example 3-3 as I go through it line by line.

This JavaScript loads a document called *index.html*, and will not work without it. You should reuse the HTML file from Chapter 2, being sure to save it as *index.html* in the same directory as the *iphone.html* you created earlier in this chapter. However, none of the links in it will work unless the targets of the links actually exist. You can create these files yourself or download the example code from the book's website (*http://www.oreilly.com/catalog/9780596805784/*). Creating *about.html*, *blog.html*, and *consulting-clinic.html* will give you a few links to play with. To do so, just duplicate *index.html* a few times and change the filename of each copy to match the related link. For added effect, you can change the content of the h2 tag in each file to match the filename. For example, the h2 in *blog.html* would be <h2>Blog</h2>.

Example 3-3. This bit of JavaScript in iphone.js converts the links on the page to Ajax requests

```
$(document).ready(function(){ ❶
    loadPage();
});
function loadPage(url) {❷
    if (url == undefined) {
        $('#container').load('index.html #header ul', hijackLinks);❸
    } else {
        $('#container').load(url + ' #content', hijackLinks);❹
    }
}
function hijackLinks() {❺
    $('#container a').click(function(e){❻
        e.preventDefault();❼
        loadPage(e.target.href);❽
    });
}
```

❶ Here I'm using jQuery's document ready function to have the browser run the loadPage() function when the DOM is complete.

❷ The loadPage() function accepts a single parameter called url, and then checks (on the next line) whether a value has been sent.

❸ If a value is not sent into the function, url will be undefined and this line will execute. This line and the following are examples of jQuery's load() function. The load() function is excellent for adding quick and dirty Ajax functionality to a page. If this line were translated into English, it would read: "Get all of the ul elements from the #header element of index.html and insert them into the #container element of the current page. When you're done, run the hijackLinks() function." Note that *index.html* refers to the home page of the site. If your home page is named differently, you'd use that filename here instead.

❹ This line is executed if the url parameter has a value. It says, in effect: "Get the #content element from the url that was passed into the loadPages() function and insert it into the #container element of the current page. When you're done, run the hijackLinks() function."

❺ Once the load() function has completed, the #container element of the current page will contain the HTML snippet that was retrieved. Then, load() will run the hijackLinks() function.

❻ On this line, hijackLinks() finds all of the links that are in the new HTML, and binds a click handler to them using the lines of code that follow. Click handlers are automatically passed an event object, which I'm capturing as the function parameter e. The event object of a clicked link contains the URL of the remote page in e.target.href.

❼ Normally, a web browser will navigate to a new page when a link is clicked. This navigation response is called the "default behavior" of the link. Since we are handling clicks and loading pages manually, we need to prevent this default behavior. On this line, I've done so by calling the built-in preventDefault() method of the event object. If I had left that line out, the browser would have dutifully left the current page and navigated to the URL of the clicked link.

❽ When the user clicks, I pass the URL of the remote page to the loadPage() function and the cycle starts all over again.

One of my favorite things about JavaScript is that you can pass a function as a parameter to another function. Although this looks weird at first, it's extremely powerful and allows you to make your code modular and reusable. If you'd like to learn more, you should check out *JavaScript: The Good Parts* by Douglas Crockford (O'Reilly). In fact, if you are working with JavaScript, you should check out everything by Douglas Crockford; you'll be glad you did.

Click handlers do not run when the page first loads; they run when the user has read some stuff on the page and decides to click a link. Assigning click handlers is like setting booby traps; you do some initial setup work for something that may or may not be triggered later.

It's worth taking a few minutes to read up on the properties of the event object that JavaScript creates in response to user actions in the browser. A good reference is located at *http://www.w3schools.com/htmldom/dom _obj_event.asp*.

Simple Bells and Whistles

With this tiny bit of HTML, CSS, and JavaScript, we have essentially turned an entire website into a single-page application. However, it still leaves quite a bit to be desired. Let's slick things up a bit.

Since we are not allowing the browser to navigate from page to page, the user will not see any indication of progress while data is loading. We need to provide some feedback to let users know that something is, in fact, happening. Without this feedback, users will wonder if they actually clicked the link or missed it, and will often start clicking all over the place in frustration. This can lead to increased server load and application instability (i.e., crashing).

 If you are testing this web application on a local network, the network speeds will be so fast you won't ever see the progress indicator. If you are using Mac OS X, you can slow all incoming web traffic by typing a couple of `ipfw` commands at the terminal. For example, these commands will slow all web traffic to 4 kilobytes per second:

```
sudo ipfw pipe 1 config bw 4KByte/s
sudo ipfw add 100 pipe 1 tcp from any to me 80
```

If you are using the Safari desktop browser to view the pages, you'll need to use your Mac's hostname or external IP address in the URL (for example, `mymac.local` rather than `localhost`). When you're done testing, delete the rule with `sudo ipfw delete 100` (you can delete all custom rules with `ipfw flush`).

Thanks to jQuery, providing this sort of feedback only takes two lines of code. We'll just append a loading `div` to the body when `loadPage()` starts, and remove the loading `div` when `hijackLinks()` is done. Example 3-4 shows a modified version of Example 3-3. The lines you need to add to *iphone.js* are shown in bold.

Example 3-4. Adding a simple progress indicator to the page

```
$(document).ready(function(){
    loadPage();
});
function loadPage(url) {
    $('body').append('<div id="progress">Loading...</div>');
    if (url == undefined) {
        $('#container').load('index.html #header ul', hijackLinks);
    } else {
        $('#container').load(url + ' #content', hijackLinks);
    }
}
function hijackLinks() {
    $('#container a').click(function(e){
        e.preventDefault();
        loadPage(e.target.href);
```

```
    });
    $('#progress').remove();
}
```

See Example 3-5 for the CSS that needs to be added to *iphone.css* to style the progress div. The result can be seen in Figure 3-1.

Figure 3-1. Without a progress indicator of some kind, your app will seem unresponsive and your users will get frustrated

Example 3-5. CSS added to iphone.css used to style the progress indicator

```
#progress {
    -webkit-border-radius: 10px;
    background-color: rgba(0,0,0,.7);
    color: white;
    font-size: 18px;
    font-weight: bold;
    height: 80px;
    left: 60px;
    line-height: 80px;
    margin: 0 auto;
    position: absolute;
    text-align: center;
    top: 120px;
    width: 200px;
}
```

My site happens to have a single h2 at the beginning of each page that would make a nice page title (see Figure 3-2). You can see this in the HTML source shown in Chapter 2. To be more iPhone-esque, I'm going to pull that title out of the content and put it in the header (see Figure 3-3). Again, jQuery to the rescue: you can just add three

Figure 3-2. Before moving the page heading to the toolbar...

Figure 3-3. ...and after moving the page heading to the toolbar

lines to the `hijackLinks()` function to make it happen. Example 3-6 shows the `hijackLinks` function with these changes.

Example 3-6. Using the h2 from the target page as the toolbar title

```
function hijackLinks() {
    $('#container a').click(function(e){
        e.preventDefault();
```

```
        loadPage(e.target.href);
    });
    var title = $('h2').html() || 'Hello!';
    $('h1').html(title);
    $('h2').remove();
    $('#progress').remove();
}
```

Note that I added the title lines before the line that removes the progress indicator. I like to remove the progress indicator as the very last action because I think it makes the application feel more responsive.

The double pipe (||) in the first line of inserted code (shown in bold) is the JavaScript logical operator OR. Translated into English, that line would read: "Set the title variable to the HTML contents of the h2 element, or to the string 'Hello!' if there is no h2 element." This is important because the first page load won't contain an h2, as we are just grabbing the nav uls.

This point probably needs some clarification. When users first load the *iphone.html* URL, they are only going to see the overall site navigation elements, as opposed to any site content. They won't see any site content until they tap a link on this initial navigation page.

A few pages on my site have titles that are longer than can fit in the header bar (Figure 3-4). I could just let the text break onto more than one line, but that would not be very iPhone-ish. Rather, I've updated the #header h1 styles such that long text will be truncated with a trailing ellipsis (see Figure 3-5 and Example 3-7). This might be my favorite little-known CSS trick.

Example 3-7. Adding an ellipsis to text that is too long for its container

```
#header h1 {
    color: #???;
    font-size: 20px;
    font-weight: bold;
    margin: 0 auto;
    padding: 10px 0;
    text-align: center;
    text-shadow: 0px 1px 0px #fff;
    max-width: 160px;
    overflow: hidden;
    white-space: nowrap;
    text-overflow: ellipsis;
}
```

Figure 3-4. Text wrapping in the toolbar is not very iPhone-ish...

Figure 3-5. ...but we can beautify it with a CSS ellipsis

Here's the rundown: `max-width: 160px` instructs the browser not to allow the `h1` element to grow wider than 160px. Then, `overflow: hidden` instructs the browser to chop off any content that extends outside of the element borders. Next, `white-space: nowrap` prevents the browser from breaking the line into two. Without this line, the `h1` would just get taller to accommodate the text at the defined width. Finally, `text-overflow: ellipsis` appends three dots to the end of any chopped-off text to indicate to users that they are not seeing the entire string.

Let's say you have an About page that is longer than the viewable area on the iPhone. The user visits the page, scrolls down to the bottom, and clicks on a link to your Contact page. If you have more than a screenful of text on your Contact page, the new data will appear with the window still scrolled all the way to the bottom.

Technically, this makes sense because we are not actually leaving the current (scrolled) page, but it's certainly confusing for the user. To rectify the situation, I have added a `scrollTo()` command to the `loadPage()` function (see Example 3-8).

Now whenever a user clicks a link, the page will first jump to the top. This has the added benefit of ensuring that the loading graphic is visible if the user clicks a link at the bottom of a long page.

Example 3-8. It's a good idea to scroll back to the top when a user navigates to a new page

```
function loadPage(url) {
    $('body').append('<div id="progress">Loading...</div>');
    scrollTo(0,0);
    if (url == undefined) {
        $('#container').load('index.html #header ul', hijackLinks);
    } else {
        $('#container').load(url + ' #content', hijackLinks);
    }
}
```

Like most sites, mine has links to external pages (i.e., pages hosted on other domains). I don't want to hijack these external links because it wouldn't make sense to inject their HTML into my iPhone-specific layout. In Example 3-9, I have added a conditional that checks the URL for the existence of my domain name. If it's found, the link is hijacked and the content is loaded into the current page; that is, Ajax is in effect. If not, the browser will navigate to the URL normally.

 You must change jonathanstark.com to the appropriate domain or hostname for your website, or the links to pages on your website will no longer be hijacked.

Example 3-9. You can allow external pages to load normally by checking the domain name of the URL

```
function hijackLinks() {
    $('#container a').click(function(e){
        var url = e.target.href;
        if (url.match(/jonathanstark.com/)) {
            e.preventDefault();
            loadPage(url);
        }
    });
    var title = $('h2').html() || 'Hello!';
    $('h1').html(title);
    $('h2').remove();
    $('#progress').remove();
}
```

The `url.match` function uses a language, regular expressions, that is often embedded within other programming languages such as JavaScript, PHP, and Perl. Although this regular expression is simple, more complex expressions can be a bit intimidating, but are well worth becoming familiar with. My favorite regex page is located at *http://www.regular -expressions.info/javascriptexample.html*.

Roll Your Own Back Button

The elephant in the room at this point is that the user has no way to navigate back to previous pages (remember that we've hijacked all the links, so the Safari page history won't work). Let's address that by adding a back button to the top-left corner of the screen. First, I'll update the JavaScript, and then I'll do the CSS.

Adding a standard iPhone-ized back button to the app means keeping track of the user's click history. To do this, we'll have to A) store the URL of the previous page so we know where to go back to, and B) store the title of the previous page so we know what label to put on the back button.

Adding this feature touches on most of the JavaScript we've written so far in this chapter, so I'll go over the entire new version of *iphone.js* line by line (see Example 3-10). The result will look like Figure 3-6.

Figure 3-6. It wouldn't be an iPhone app without a glossy, left-arrow back button

Example 3-10. Expanding the existing JavaScript example to include support for a back button

```
var hist = [];❶
var startUrl = 'index.html';❷
```

```
$(document).ready(function(){❸
    loadPage(startUrl);
});
function loadPage(url) {
    $('body').append('<div id="progress">Loading...</div>');❹
    scrollTo(0,0);
    if (url == startUrl) {❺
        var element = ' #header ul';
    } else {
        var element = ' #content';
    }
    $('#container').load(url + element, function(){❻
        var title = $('h2').html() || 'Hello!';
        $('h1').html(title);
        $('h2').remove();
        $('.leftButton').remove();❼
        hist.unshift({'url':url, 'title':title});❽
        if (hist.length > 1) {❾
            $('#header').append('<div class="leftButton">'+hist[1].title+'</div>');❿
            $('#header .leftButton').click(function(){⓫
                var thisPage = hist.shift();⓬
                var previousPage = hist.shift();
                loadPage(previousPage.url);
            });
        }
        $('#container a').click(function(e){⓭
            var url = e.target.href;
            if (url.match(/jonathanstark.com/)) {⓮
                e.preventDefault();
                loadPage(url);
            }
        });
        $('#progress').remove();
    });
}
```

❶ On this line, I'm initializing a variable named hist as an empty array. Since I've defined it outside of any functions, it exists in the global scope and will be available everywhere in the page. Note that I didn't use the full word history as my variable name because that is a predefined object property in JavaScript and should be avoided in your own code.

❷ Here I'm defining the relative URL of the remote page to load when the user first visits *iphone.html*. You might recall from earlier examples that I just checked for url == undefined to handle the first page load, but in this example we are going to use the start page in a few places. Therefore, it makes sense to define it globally.

❸ This line and the next make up the document ready function definition. Note that unlike previous examples, I'm passing the start page to the loadPage() function.

❹ On to the loadPage() function. This line and the next are verbatim from previous examples.

❺ This `if...else` statement determines which elements to load from the remote page. For example, if we want the start page, we grab the `ul`s from the header; otherwise, we grab the content `div`.

❻ On this line, the URL parameter and the appropriate source element are concatenated as the first parameter passed to the load function. As for the second parameter, I'm passing an *anonymous function* (an unnamed function that is defined inline) directly. As we go through the anonymous function, you'll notice a strong resemblance to the `hijackLinks()` function, which this anonymous function has replaced. For example, the following three lines are identical to previous examples.

❼ On this line, I'm removing the `.leftButton` object from the page. (This might seem weird because I haven't yet added it to the page; we'll be adding it a couple steps down.)

❽ Here I'm using the built-in `unshift` method of the JavaScript array to add an object to the beginning of the `hist` array. The object I'm adding has two properties, `url` and `title`, which are the two pieces of information we need to support the back button display and behavior.

❾ On this line, I'm using the built-in `length` method of the JavaScript array to find out how many objects are in the history array. If there is only one object in the history array, it means that the user is on the first page, and therefore we don't need to display a back button. However, if there is more than one object in the `hist` array, we need to add a button to the header.

❿ Next, I'm adding that `.leftButton` I mentioned earlier. The text of the button will be the same as the title of the page before the current page, which is what I'm accessing with the `hist[1].title` code. JavaScript arrays are zero-based, so the first item in the array (the current page) has an index of 0. In other words, index 0 is the current page, index 1 is the previous page, index 2 is the page before that, and so on.

⓫ In this block of code, I'm binding an anonymous function to the click handler of the back button. Remember, click handler code executes when the user clicks, not when the page loads. So, after the page loads and the user clicks to go back, the code inside this function will run.

⓬ This line and the next use the built-in `shift` method of the array to remove the first two items from the `hist` array, and the last line in the function sends the URL of the previous page to the `loadPage()` function.

⓭ The remaining lines were copied exactly from previous examples, so I won't rehash them here.

⓮ This is the URL matching code introduced earlier in this chapter. Remember to replace `jonathanstark.com` with part of your website's domain or hostname, or none of the local links will be hijacked and loaded into the page.

Please visit *http://www.hunlock.com/blogs/Mastering_Javascript_Ar rays* for a full listing of JavaScript array functions with descriptions and examples.

Now that we have our back button, all that remains is to purty it up with some CSS (see Example 3-11). I start off by styling the text with `font-weight`, `text-align`, `line-height`, `color`, and `text-shadow`. I continue by placing the `div` precisely where I want it on the page with `position`, `top`, and `left`. Then, I make sure that long text on the button label will truncate with an ellipsis using `max-width`, `white-space`, `overflow`, and `text-overflow`. Finally, I apply a graphic with `border-width` and `-webkit-border-image`. Unlike my earlier border image example, this image has a different width for the left and right borders, because the image is made asymmetrical by the arrowhead on the left side.

Don't forget that you'll need an image for this button. You'll need to save it as *back_button.png* in the *images* folder underneath the folder that holds your HTML file. See "Adding Basic Behavior with jQuery" on page 24 for tips on finding or creating your own button images.

Example 3-11. Add the following to iphone.css to beautify the back button with a border image

```
#header div.leftButton {
    font-weight: bold;
    text-align: center;
    line-height: 28px;
    color: white;
    text-shadow: rgba(0,0,0,0.6) 0px -1px 0px;
    position: absolute;
    top: 7px;
    left: 6px;
    max-width: 50px;
    white-space: nowrap;
    overflow: hidden;
    text-overflow: ellipsis;
    border-width: 0 8px 0 14px;
    -webkit-border-image: url(images/back_button.png) 0 8 0 14;
}
```

By default, Mobile Safari briefly displays a translucent gray box over clickable objects that have been tapped (Figure 3-7). Since our back button is not rectangular, this effect looks a little lame, but removing it is easy and makes the app look much better. Mobile Safari supports a property called `-webkit-tap-highlight-color` that allows you to change the default to whatever color you like. I want to remove the highlight completely, which I've done here by setting the tap highlight to a fully transparent color (see Example 3-12).

Figure 3-7. By default, Mobile Safari displays a translucent gray box over clickable objects that have been tapped

Example 3-12. Add the following to iphone.css to remove the default tap highlight from Mobile Safari

```
#header div.leftButton {
    font-weight: bold;
    text-align: center;
    line-height: 28px;
    color: white;
    text-shadow: rgba(0,0,0,0.6) 0px -1px 0px;
    position: absolute;
    top: 7px;
    left: 6px;
    max-width: 50px;
    white-space: nowrap;
    overflow: hidden;
    text-overflow: ellipsis;
    border-width: 0 8px 0 14px;
    -webkit-border-image: url(images/back_button.png) 0 8 0 14;
    -webkit-tap-highlight-color: rgba(0,0,0,0);
}
```

In the case of the back button, there can be at least a second or two of delay before the content from the previous page appears. To avoid frustration, I want the button to look clicked the instant it's tapped. In a desktop browser, this would be a simple process; you'd just add a declaration to your CSS using the `:active` pseudoclass to specify an alternate style for the object that was clicked. I don't know whether it's a bug or a feature, but this approach does not work on the iPhone; the `:active` style is ignored.

I toyed around with combinations of `:active` and `:hover`, which brought me some success with non-Ajax apps. However, with an Ajax app like the one we are using here, the :hover style is sticky (i.e., the button appears to remain "clicked" even after the finger is removed).

Fortunately, the fix is pretty simple. I use jQuery to add the class clicked to the button when the user taps it. I've opted to apply a darker version of the button image to the button in the example (see Figure 3-8 and Example 3-13). You'll need to make sure you have a button image called *back_button_clicked.png* in the *images* subfolder. See "Adding Basic Behavior with jQuery" on page 24 for tips on finding or creating your own button images.

Figure 3-8. It's a subtle difference, but the clicked back button is a bit darker than the default state

Example 3-13. Add the following to iphone.css to make the back button look clicked the moment the user taps it

```
#header div.leftButton.clicked {
    -webkit-border-image: url(images/back_button_clicked.png) 0 8 0 14;
}
```

 Since I'm using an image for the clicked style, it would be smart to preload the image. Otherwise, the unclicked button graphic will disappear the first time it's tapped while the clicked graphic downloads. I'll cover image preloading in the next chapter.

With the CSS in place, I can now update the portion of *iphone.js* that assigns the click handler to the back button. First, I add a variable, e, to the anonymous function in order to capture the incoming click event. Then, I wrap the event target in a jQuery selector and call jQuery's addClass() function to assign my clicked CSS class to the button:

```
$('#header .leftButton').click(function(e){
    $(e.target).addClass('clicked');
    var thisPage = hist.shift();
    var previousPage = hist.shift();
    loadPage(previousPage.url);
});
```

 A special note to any CSS gurus in the crowd: the CSS Sprite technique—
popularized by A List Apart—is not an option in this case because it
requires setting offsets for the image. Image offsets are not supported
by the -webkit-border-image property.

Adding an Icon to the Home Screen

Hopefully users will want to add an icon for your web app (called a "Web Clip icon")
to their home screens. They do this by tapping the plus button at the bottom of the
Safari window (Figure 3-9), tapping Add to Home Screen (Figure 3-10), and clicking
the Add button (Figure 3-11). By default, the iPhone will create this icon by thumb-
nailing the current page (including position and zoom) and applying rounded corners
and a glossy effect (Figure 3-12).

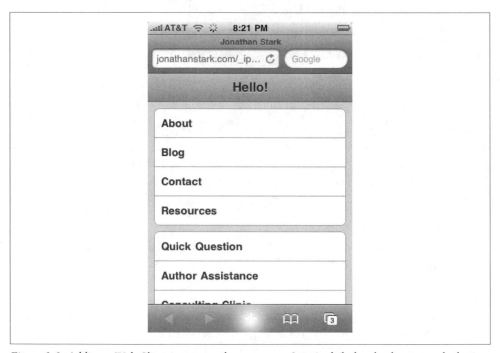

*Figure 3-9. Adding a Web Clip icon to your home screen, Step 1: click the plus button at the bottom
of the Safari window*

Figure 3-10. Step 2: click the "Add to Home Screen" button in the dialog

Figure 3-11. Step 3: click the "Add" button in the "Add to Home" panel

Figure 3-12. Step 4: a 57 × 57 pixel image will show up on the home screen

To customize the home screen image, the cool kids provide a custom Web Clip icon. The simplest way to do this is to specify a single icon for your entire site by uploading a file named *apple-touch-icon.png* to your web root. The file should be 57 pixels square, and without gloss or rounded corners because the iPhone will add these automatically. If you don't want the iPhone to add effects to your Web Clip icon, change the name of the file to *apple-touch-icon-precomposed.png*.

In some cases, you may want to provide a Web Clip icon for a page that is different from the rest of your site. You can do this by adding one of the following lines to the `head` section of the "traffic cop" HTML document, *iphone.html* (replacing `myCustomIcon.png` with the absolute or relative path to the image):

```
<link rel="apple-touch-icon" href="myCustomIcon.png" />

<link rel="apple-touch-icon-precomposed" href="myCustomIcon.png" />
```

 If you are going to use precomposed images, make the corner radius 10 pixels or more; otherwise, the iPhone will round the corners to 10 pixels. In either case, using precomposed images does suppress the addition of the glossy effect.

Full Screen Mode

Feel like reclaiming a quarter of the available vertical space from Mobile Safari (104 pixels, to be precise)? Add the following line to the `head` section of the "traffic cop" HTML document, *iphone.html*, and your web app will display in full screen mode when launched from the Web Clip icon:

```
<meta name="apple-mobile-web-app-capable" content="yes" />
```

I would've told you about this feature earlier, but it's only useful once you have hijacked all of your hyperlinks with Ajax. As soon as a user clicks on a nonhijacked link—one that actually navigates to a new page—Mobile Safari will launch and load the page normally. This behavior is perfect for the example we've been working with because external links (Amazon, Twitter, Facebook, etc.) will open in Safari.

Changing the Status Bar

Once you've added the `apple-mobile-web-app-capable` meta tag, you have the option to control the background color of the 20-pixel status bar at the top of the screen using the `apple-mobile-web-app-status-bar-style` meta tag. The normal gray Safari status bar is the default, or you can change it to `black` (see Figure 3-13). You can also set it to `black-translucent`, which makes it partially transparent and additionally removes it from the document flow. In other words, your content will be shifted up by 20 pixels and behind the status bar when the page first loads, so you might have to position your header a little lower to compensate:

```
<meta name="apple-mobile-web-app-status-bar-style" content="black" />
```

 Changes to the status bar style will only take effect when the app is launched in full screen mode.

Figure 3-13. Full screen mode gives you about 25% more screen real estate and allows you to customize the appearance of the status bar

Providing a Custom Startup Graphic

When an app is launched in full screen mode, the user is presented with a screenshot of the app while the first page is loading. I'm not a fan of this because it looks like the app is ready to be interacted with, when in reality tapping a link will do nothing. Furthermore, the screenshot is based on the last page from the user's previous visit, scrolled to wherever he left off—not very attractive.

Fortunately, Mobile Safari allows us to define a startup graphic that will be displayed while the page is loading. To add a custom startup graphic, create a 320px × 460px PNG file and place it in the same directory with *iphone.html*. Next, add the following line to the head section of *iphone.html* (you'd replace myCustomStartupGraphic.png with the absolute or relative path to your image):

```
<link rel="apple-touch-startup-image" href="myCustomStartupGraphic.png" />
```

The next time we launch our app from the Web Clip icon, the default loading behavior will take place while the new custom graphic is downloaded. On the subsequent launch, the custom startup graphic will be displayed (Figure 3-14).

Figure 3-14. Providing a custom startup graphic for an app launched in full screen mode

What You've Learned

In this chapter, you've learned how to convert a normal website into a full-screen Ajax application, complete with progress indicators, a native-looking back button, and a custom Web Clip icon. In the next chapter, you'll learn how to make your app come alive by adding native user interface animations. That's right; here comes the fun stuff!

CHAPTER 4

Animation

iPhone apps have a number of distinctive animation characteristics that add context and meaning for the user. For example, pages slide left as you drill down through links, and slide right as you navigate back. In this chapter, you'll learn how to add characteristic behaviors like sliding, page flip, and more to your web app. These changes, in combination with Ajax and full screen mode, will make your web app almost indistinguishable from a native application.

With a Little Help from Our Friend

I'll be honest: making a web page animate like a typical native iPhone app is hard. Fortunately, an enterprising young lad from Philly named David Kaneda has written a JavaScript library called jQTouch that makes mobile web development a whole lot easier. jQTouch is an open source jQuery plug-in that handles virtually everything we learned in the previous chapter, as well as a boatload of much more complex stuff that would be truly painful to write from scratch.

 You can download the latest version of jQTouch from *http://jqtouch .com/*.

Sliding Home

We are going to build a simple calorie-tracking application called Kilo that allows the user to add and delete food entries for a given date. All told, there will be five panels: Home, Settings, Dates, Date, and New Entry. We'll start off with two panels and work our way up as we go.

I'll be assigning CSS classes to some of the HTML elements (`toolbar`, `edgetoedge`, `arrow`, `button`, `back`, etc.). In every case, these classes correspond to predefined CSS class selectors that exist in the default jQTouch theme. Bear in mind that you can create and use your own classes by modifying existing jQTouch themes or building your own from scratch; I'm just using the defaults.

To begin, let's create a file named *index.html* and add the HTML shown in Example 4-1 for the Home and About panels.

Figure 4-1. Kilo before jQTouch...

Example 4-1. HTML for the Home and About panels in index.html

```html
<html>
    <head>
        <title>Kilo</title>
    </head>
    <body>
        <div id="home">❶
            <div class="toolbar">❷
                <h1>Kilo</h1>
            </div>
            <ul class="edgetoedge">❸
                <li class="arrow"><a href="#about">About</a></li>❹
            </ul>
        </div>
        <div id="about">
            <div class="toolbar">
                <h1>About</h1>
                <a class="button back" href="#">Back</a>❺
```

```
            </div>
            <div>
                <p>Kilo gives you easy access to your food diary.</p>
            </div>
        </div>
    </body>
</html>
```

The HTML here basically amounts to a head with a title, and a body with two children, both divs:

❶ This div (as well as the about div that appears a few lines down) will become a panel in the application by virtue of the fact that it is a direct descendant of the body.

❷ Inside each panel div, there is a div with a class of toolbar. This toolbar class is specifically predefined in the jQTouch themes to style an element like a traditional iPhone toolbar.

❸ This unordered list tag has the class edgetoedge. The edgetoedge class tells jQTouch to stretch the list all the way from left to right in the viewable area.

❹ On this line there is an li that contains a link with its href pointing at the About panel. Including the arrow class to the li is optional; doing so will add a chevron to the right side of the item in the list.

❺ The toolbar elements each contain a single h1 element that will become the panel title. On this line, there is a link with the classes button and back, which tell jQTouch to make the button look and act like a back button.

Note that the href on the back button is set to #. Normally, this would tell the browser to return to the top of the current document. But when using jQTouch, it navigates back to the previous panel instead. In more advanced scenarios, you might want to use a specific anchor, such as #home, which would instruct the back button to navigate to a particular panel regardless of what the previous panel was.

With the basic HTML in place, it's time to add jQTouch to the party. Once you've downloaded jQTouch and unzipped it in the same directory as the HTML document, you just add a few lines of code to the head of your page (Example 4-2).

For this and other examples in this book, you will need to download jQTouch from *http://jqtouch.com*, unzip it, and move the *jqtouch* and *themes* directories into the same directory as your HTML document. You will also need to go into the *jqtouch* directory and rename the jQuery JavaScript file (such as *jquery.1.3.2.min.js*) to *jquery.js*.

Example 4-2. Adding these lines to the head of your document will activate jQTouch

```
<link type="text/css" rel="stylesheet" media="screen" href="jqtouch/jqtouch.css">❶
<link type="text/css" rel="stylesheet" media="screen" href="themes/jqt/theme.css">❷
<script type="text/javascript" src="jqtouch/jquery.js"></script>❸
<script type="text/javascript" src="jqtouch/jqtouch.js"></script>❹
<script type="text/javascript">❺
    var jQT = $.jQTouch({
        icon: 'kilo.png',
        statusBar: 'black'
    });
</script>
```

❶ I'm including the *jqtouch.css* file. This file defines some hardcore structural design rules that are very specific to handling animations, orientation, and other iPhone-specific minutiae. This file is required and there should be no reason for you to edit it.

❷ I'm including the CSS for my selected theme, in this case, the "jqt" theme, which comes with jQTouch. The classes that I've been using in the HTML correspond to CSS selectors in this document. jQTouch comes with two themes available by default. You can also make your own by duplicating a default theme and making changes to it, or writing a new one from scratch.

❸ jQTouch requires jQuery, so I include that here. jQTouch comes with its own copy of jQuery, but you can link to another copy if you prefer.

❹ This is where I include jQTouch itself. Note that you have to include jQTouch after jQuery, or nothing's going to work.

❺ This brings us to the script block where I initialize the jQTouch object and send in two property values: `icon` and `statusBar`.

jQTouch exposes several properties that allow you to customize the behavior and appearance of your app. You'll see several throughout the course of this book, and they are all optional. However, you'll pretty much always be using at least a few of them.

In this case, `icon` tells jQTouch where to look for the custom Web Clip icon, and `statusBar` controls the color of the 20px strip at the top of the app in full screen mode.

 By the way, jQTouch assumes that you want the app to run in full screen mode because, hey...that's how you roll. If you'd prefer to disallow full screen mode, you can add `fullScreen: false` to the property list.

The difference between the application before jQTouch (Figure 4-1) and after (Figure 4-2) is dramatic, but the truly astonishing thing is that you've just added gorgeous left/right sliding to your app with 10 lines of code. What's more, you've also enabled

Figure 4-2. ...and Kilo after jQTouch

full screen mode, defined a custom status bar color, and linked to your Web Clip icon. jQTouch is completely sick, and we're just getting started.

Adding the Dates Panel

Let's now add the Dates panel. The Dates panel will have a list of relative dates beginning with Today and going back to 5 days ago (Figure 4-3). Add the HTML for the Dates panel (shown in Example 4-3) right after the About panel, just before the closing `</body>`.

Example 4-3. The HTML for the Dates panel

```
<div id="dates">
    <div class="toolbar">
        <h1>Dates</h1>
        <a class="button back" href="#">Back</a>
    </div>
    <ul class="edgetoedge">
        <li class="arrow"><a id="0" href="#date">Today</a></li>
        <li class="arrow"><a id="1" href="#date">Yesterday</a></li>
        <li class="arrow"><a id="2" href="#date">2 Days Ago</a></li>
        <li class="arrow"><a id="3" href="#date">3 Days Ago</a></li>
        <li class="arrow"><a id="4" href="#date">4 Days Ago</a></li>
        <li class="arrow"><a id="5" href="#date">5 Days Ago</a></li>
    </ul>
</div>
```

Figure 4-3. The Dates panel consists of a toolbar with a back button and a clickable list of relative dates

Like the About panel, the Dates panel has a toolbar with a title and back button. After the toolbar, there is an unordered `edgetoedge` list of links. Notice that all of the links have unique `id`s (0 through 5) but the same `href` (`#date`)—more on that in a bit.

Next, you have to update the Home panel with a link to the Dates panel. Add the following line to the Home panel in *index.html*:

```
<div id="home">
    <div class="toolbar">
        <h1>Kilo</h1>
    </div>
    <ul class="edgetoedge">
        <li class="arrow"><a href="#dates">Dates</a></li>
        <li class="arrow"><a href="#about">About</a></li>
    </ul>
</div>
```

And just like that, we've added a new panel to the app (see Figure 4-4). Clicking on an item on the Dates panel doesn't do anything yet. Let's rectify that situation by adding the Date panel.

Adding the Date Panel

The Date panel looks a lot like the previous panels, with a couple of exceptions (refer to Example 4-4). Add the HTML for the Date panel right after the Dates panel, just before the closing `</body>`.

Figure 4-4. The Home panel now has a link to the Dates panel

Example 4-4. The HTML for the Date panel

```
<div id="date">
    <div class="toolbar">
        <h1>Date</h1>
        <a class="button back" href="#">Back</a>
        <a class="button slideup" href="#createEntry">+</a>❶
    </div>
    <ul class="edgetoedge">
        <li id="entryTemplate" class="entry" style="display:none">❷
            <span class="label">Label</span>
            <span class="calories">000</span>
            <span class="delete">Delete</span>
        </li>
    </ul>
</div>
```

❶ The Date panel toolbar has an additional button. When clicked, this button will display the New Entry panel (which we have not yet built). I've given the link a class of `slideup`, which tells jQTouch that we want the target panel to slide up from the bottom of the screen, rather than horizontally like typical navigation.

❷ The other unusual aspect of this panel is that I've defined a list item with the style set to `display:none`, effectively making it invisible.

As you'll see in a bit, I'm going to use this invisible list item as a template to display entries once they are created. At this point, there are no entries, so the panel will be empty aside from the toolbar.

Now that you've added the Date panel, clicking any item on the Dates panel will slide the empty Date panel (Figure 4-5) into view.

Figure 4-5. Apart from the toolbar, the Date panel is empty to begin with

Adding the New Entry Panel

Example 4-5 shows the source code for the New Entry panel. Add this code of *index.html*, just before the closing **</body>**.

Example 4-5. The HTML for the New Entry panel

```
<div id="createEntry">
    <div class="toolbar">
        <h1>New Entry</h1>
        <a class="button cancel" href="#">Cancel</a>❶
    </div>
    <form method="post">❷
        <ul>
            <li><input type="text" placeholder="Food" name="food" id="food"
                autocapitalize="off" autocorrect="off" autocomplete="off" /></li>
            <li><input type="text" placeholder="Calories" name="calories" id="calories"
                autocapitalize="off" autocorrect="off" autocomplete="off" /></li>
            <li><input type="submit" class="submit" name="action"
                value="Save Entry" /></li>❸
        </ul>
    </form>
</div>
```

❶ The first thing to point out about the New Entry panel is that instead of having a back button, it has a cancel button.

Cancel buttons in jQTouch behave just like back buttons, in that they remove the current page from view using the reverse animation of the way it came into view. However, unlike back buttons, cancel buttons are not shaped like a left arrow.

I used a cancel button for the New Entry panel because it slides up on the way in and will therefore slide down on the way out. It would be counterintuitive to click a left-pointing back button and then have the panel slide down.

❷ This HTML form contains an unordered list of three items: two text fields and a submit button. Embedding form controls in an li allows the jqt theme to style the form as shown in Figure 4-6.

Each of the text inputs has quite a few defined attributes:

type
: Defines the form control to be a single-line text entry field.

placeholder
: A string of text to display in the form input when the input is empty.

name
: The name that will be associated with the value provided by the user when the form is submitted.

id
: A unique identifier for the element in the context of the entire page.

autocapitalize
: A Mobile Safari–specific setting that allows you to turn off the default autocapitalization feature.

autocorrect
: A Mobile Safari–specific setting that allows you to turn off the default spellcheck feature.

autocomplete
: Setting that allows you to turn off the autocomplete feature of Mobile Safari.

❸ The class attribute of the submit input button needs explanation. The iPhone will display a keyboard whenever your cursor is in a field. The keyboard has a Go button in the bottom-right corner that submits the form when clicked. When you are hijacking the submit function as we are doing here, submitting from the Go button on the keyboard does not remove the cursor from the active field, and therefore the keyboard does not slide out of view. To remedy this, jQTouch offers a convenience method that automatically removes the cursor from the active field when a form is submitted. To take advantage of this feature, you just add the submit class to the submit element of the form.

Figure 4-7 shows the New Entry form in action. At this point, I've done nothing to actually save the entry when the user clicks Save Entry. We'll cover that in Chapter 5.

Figure 4-6. The jqt theme does a nice job styling form elements

Figure 4-7. Keyboard data entry with the New Entry form

Adding the Settings Panel

We haven't yet created a button that will allow users to navigate to the Settings panel, so let's add one to the toolbar on the Home panel (see Figure 4-8). All it takes is a single line of HTML, shown in bold:

```
<div id="home">
    <div class="toolbar">
        <h1>Kilo</h1>
        <a class="button flip" href="#settings">Settings</a>❶
    </div>
    <ul class="edgetoedge">
        <li class="arrow"><a href="#dates">Dates</a></li>
        <li class="arrow"><a href="#about">About</a></li>
    </ul>
</div>
```

❶ This is the line of HTML that adds the button. Notice that I've assigned the `flip` class to the link. The `flip` class instructs jQTouch to transition from the Home panel to the Settings panel by rotating the page on its vertical axis. To add an extra dimension to the process, the page actually zooms out a bit during the animation, similar to the default Weather app on the iPhone. Fancy, no?

Figure 4-8. The Settings button added to the toolbar on the Home panel

In comparison with the New Entry panel, the HTML for the Settings panel is going to look pretty familiar (Example 4-6). There is one more text input and some of the attributes have been omitted or have different values, but conceptually they are identical. Add this to your HTML document just as you've done for the other panels. When you're done, the Settings panel should look like Figure 4-9.

As with the New Entry form, the Settings form does not currently save any of the information associated with it. Its submission handler will be described in the next chapter.

Figure 4-9. The Settings panel

Example 4-6. The HTML for the Settings panel

```
<div id="settings">
    <div class="toolbar">
        <h1>Settings</h1>
        <a class="button cancel" href="#">Cancel</a>
    </div>
    <form method="post">
        <ul>
            <li><input placeholder="Age" type="text" name="age" id="age" /></li>
            <li><input placeholder="Weight" type="text" name="weight" id="weight" /></li>
            <li><input placeholder="Budget" type="text" name="budget" id="budget" /></li>
            <li><input type="submit" class="submit" name="action"
                value="Save Changes" /></li>
        </ul>
    </form>
</div>
```

Putting It All Together

So there you have it. With fewer than 100 lines of code, we've created an iPhone-esque
UI for a five-panel application, complete with three different page transition animations. Not too shabby, right? See Example 4-7 for a complete listing of the final HTML.

Example 4-7. The complete HTML listing for the five-panel UI

```
<html>
    <head>
        <title>Kilo</title>
        <link type="text/css" rel="stylesheet" media="screen" href="jqtouch/jqtouch.css">
```

```
<link type="text/css" rel="stylesheet" media="screen"
    href="themes/jqt/theme.css">
<script type="text/javascript" src="jqtouch/jquery.js"></script>
<script type="text/javascript" src="jqtouch/jqtouch.js"></script>
<script type="text/javascript">
    var jQT = $.jQTouch({
        icon: 'kilo.png',
        statusBar: 'black'
    });
</script>
</head>
<body>
    <div id="home">
        <div class="toolbar">
            <h1>Kilo</h1>
            <a class="button flip" href="#settings">Settings</a>
        </div>
        <ul class="edgetoedge">
            <li class="arrow"><a href="#dates">Dates</a></li>
            <li class="arrow"><a href="#about">About</a></li>
        </ul>
    </div>
    <div id="about">
        <div class="toolbar">
            <h1>About</h1>
            <a class="button back" href="#">Back</a>
        </div>
        <div>
            <p>Kilo gives you easy access to your food diary.</p>
        </div>
    </div>
    <div id="dates">
        <div class="toolbar">
            <h1>Dates</h1>
            <a class="button back" href="#">Back</a>
        </div>
        <ul class="edgetoedge">
            <li class="arrow"><a id="0" href="#date">Today</a></li>
            <li class="arrow"><a id="1" href="#date">Yesterday</a></li>
            <li class="arrow"><a id="2" href="#date">2 Days Ago</a></li>
            <li class="arrow"><a id="3" href="#date">3 Days Ago</a></li>
            <li class="arrow"><a id="4" href="#date">4 Days Ago</a></li>
            <li class="arrow"><a id="5" href="#date">5 Days Ago</a></li>
        </ul>
    </div>
    <div id="date">
        <div class="toolbar">
            <h1>Date</h1>
            <a class="button back" href="#">Back</a>
            <a class="button slideup" href="#createEntry">+</a>
        </div>
        <ul class="edgetoedge">
            <li id="entryTemplate" class="entry" style="display:none">
                <span class="label">Label</span>
                <span class="calories">000</span>
```

```
                    <span class="delete">Delete</span>
                </li>
            </ul>
        </div>
        <div id="createEntry">
            <div class="toolbar">
                <h1>New Entry</h1>
                <a class="button cancel" href="#">Cancel</a>
            </div>
            <form method="post">
                <ul>
                    <li><input type="text" placeholder="Food"
                        name="food" id="food" autocapitalize="off"
                        autocorrect="off" autocomplete="off" /></li>
                    <li><input type="text" placeholder="Calories"
                        name="calories" id="calories" autocapitalize="off"
                        autocorrect="off" autocomplete="off" /></li>
                    <li><input type="submit" class="submit" name="action"
                        value="Save Entry" /></li>
                </ul>
            </form>
        </div>
        <div id="settings">
            <div class="toolbar">
                <h1>Settings</h1>
                <a class="button cancel" href="#">Cancel</a>
            </div>
            <form method="post">
                <ul>
                    <li><input placeholder="Age" type="text" name="age" id="age" /></li>
                    <li><input placeholder="Weight" type="text" name="weight"
                        id="weight" /></li>
                    <li><input placeholder="Budget" type="text" name="budget"
                        id="budget" /></li>
                    <li><input type="submit" class="submit" name="action"
                        value="Save Changes" /></li>
                </ul>
            </form>
        </div>
    </body>
</html>
```

Customizing jQTouch

jQTouch allows you to customize its default behavior by sending a variety of property settings into the constructor. We've seen this previously with `icon` and `statusBar`, but there are many others that you should be aware of. See Table 4-1.

Table 4-1. jQTouch customization options

Property	Default	Expects	Notes
addGlossToIcon	true	true or false	If set to true, allow iPhone to add gloss to your Web Clip icon.

Property	Default	Expects	Notes
backSelector	`'.back, .cancel, .goback'`	Any valid CSS selector; separate multiple values with a comma	Defines elements that will trigger the "back" behavior of jQTouch when tapped. When the back behavior is invoked, the current panel moves off screen with a reverse animation and is removed from history.
cacheGetRequests	`true`	`true` or `false`	If set to `true`, automatically caches GET requests, so subsequent clicks reference the already loaded data.
cubeSelector	`'.cube'`	Any valid CSS selector; separate multiple values with a comma	Defines elements that will trigger a cube animation from the current panel to the target panel.
dissolveSelector	`'.dissolve'`	Any valid CSS selector; separate multiple values with a comma	Defines elements that will trigger a dissolve animation from the current panel to the target panel.
fadeSelector	`'.fade'`	Any valid CSS selector; separate multiple values with a comma	Defines elements that will trigger a fade animation from the current panel to the target panel.
fixedViewport	`true`	`true` or `false`	If set to `true`, prevents users from being able to zoom in or out on the page.
flipSelector	`'.flip'`	Any valid CSS selector; separate multiple values with a comma	Defines elements that will trigger a flip animation from the current panel to the target panel.
formSelector	`'form'`	Any valid CSS selector; separate multiple values with a comma	Defines elements that should be styled as a form by the CSS theme.
fullScreen	`true`	`true` or `false`	When set to `true`, your app will open in full screen mode when launched from the user's home screen. Has no effect on the display if the app is running in Mobile Safari.
fullScreenClass	`'fullscreen'`	String	Class name that will be applied to the body when the app is launched in full screen mode. Allows you to write custom

Property	Default	Expects	Notes
			CSS that only executes in full screen mode.
icon	null	null or a relative or absolute path to a 57 × 57 px png image file	The Web Clip icon for your app. This is the image that will be displayed when a user saves your app to her home screen.
popSelector	'.pop'	Any valid CSS selector; separate multiple values with a comma	Defines elements that will trigger a pop animation from the current panel to the target panel.
preloadImages	false	An array of image paths to load before page loads	Ex: ['images/link_over.png', 'images/link_select.png'].
slideInSelector	'ul li a'	Any valid CSS selector; separate multiple values with a comma	Defines elements that will trigger a slide left animation from the current panel to the target panel.
slideupSelector	'.slideup'	Any valid CSS selector; separate multiple values with a comma	Defines elements that will cause the target panel to slide up into view in front of the current panel.
startupScreen	null	null or a relative or absolute path to an image file	Pass a relative or absolute path to a 320px × 460px startup screen for full-screen apps. Use a 320px × 480px image if you set statusBar to black-translucent.
statusBar	'default'	default, black-translu cent, black	Defines the appearance of the 20-pixel status bar at the top of the window in an app launched in full screen mode.
submitSelector	'.submit'	Any valid CSS selector; separate multiple values with a comma	Selector that, when clicked, will submit its parent form (and close keyboard if open).
swapSelector	'.swap'	Any valid CSS selector; separate multiple	Defines elements that will cause the target panel to swap into view in front of the current panel.

Property	Default	Expects	Notes
		values with a comma	
useAnimations	true	true or false	Set to `false` to disable all animations.

What You've Learned

In this chapter, you've learned how to add native-looking animations to a web app using jQTouch. In the next chapter, you'll learn how to use the new local storage and client-side database features of HTML5 to add persistent data storage to your app.

CHAPTER 5

Client-Side Data Storage

Most software applications need to store data in some sort of persistent fashion in order to be useful. When it comes to web apps, this task has traditionally been handled either with a server-side database or cookies set in the browser. With the advent of HTML5, web developers now have a few more options: localStorage, sessionStorage, and client-side databases.

localStorage and sessionStorage

localStorage and sessionStorage (collectively referred to as key/value storage) are very similar to cookies in that they allow you to use JavaScript to set name/value pairs that you can then retrieve across multiple page reloads.

Unlike cookies, however, localStorage and sessionStorage data is not sent across the wire with the browser request—it lives entirely in the client. Therefore, it's feasible to store much more data than you would want to with cookies.

 At the time of this writing, browser size limits for localStorage and sessionStorage are still in flux.

Functionally, localStorage and sessionStorage are the same. They differ only in terms of persistence and scope:

`localStorage`
> Data is saved even after the window is closed and is available to all windows (or tabs) that are loaded from the same source (must be the same domain name, protocol, and port). This is useful for things like application preferences.

`sessionStorage`

Data is stored with the window object. Other windows/tabs are not aware of the values, and the data is discarded when the window/tab is closed. Useful for window-specific state like active tab highlight, or the sort order of a table.

In any of the following examples, you can substitute `sessionStorage` anywhere you see `localStorage`.

Setting a value is as simple as:

```
localStorage.setItem('age', 40);
```

Accessing a stored value is equally simple:

```
var age = localStorage.getItem('age');
```

You can delete a specific key/value pair from storage with:

```
localStorage.removeItem('age');
```

Or, you can delete all key/value pairs like so:

```
localStorage.clear();
```

Assuming that your keys are valid JavaScript tokens (no spaces, no punctuation other than underscores, etc.), you can use this alternate syntax:

```
localStorage.age = 40 // Set the value of age
var age = localStorage.age; // Get the value of age
delete localStorage.age; // Remove age from storage
```

The localStorage and sessionStorage keys are stored separately. If you use the same key name in each, they will not conflict with each other.

Saving User Settings to localStorage

On to a practical example. Let's update the Settings panel of the example app we started working on in Chapter 4 to store the form values in localStorage.

We are going to be writing a fair amount of JavaScript in this chapter, and I don't want to jam it all in the head section of our HTML document. To keep our code organized, I'm going to create a file called *kilo.js* and update the head of my HTML document with a reference to it:

```
<head>
    <title>Kilo</title>
    <link type="text/css" rel="stylesheet" media="screen" href="jqtouch/jqtouch.css">
    <link type="text/css" rel="stylesheet" media="screen"
```

```
                href="themes/jqt/theme.css">
    <script type="text/javascript" src="jqtouch/jquery.js"></script>
    <script type="text/javascript" src="jqtouch/jqtouch.js"></script>
    <script type="text/javascript" src="kilo.js"></script>
</head>
```

Alert readers will notice that I've also removed the jQTouch constructor from the head of the HTML document. It's not gone, though; I just moved it into *kilo.js*. So be sure you've removed that from your main HTML file, create the *kilo.js* file in the same directory with the following contents, and then reload the main HTML document in your browser to make sure it's still working:

```
var jQT = $.jQTouch({
    icon: 'kilo.png',
    statusBar: 'black'
});
```

I need to override the submit action of the Settings form and replace it with a custom function called `saveSettings()`. Thanks to jQuery, I can accomplish this with a single line of code, which I'll place in the document ready function. Add the following to *kilo.js*:

```
$(document).ready(function(){
    $('#settings form').submit(saveSettings);
});
```

The net result of this is that when the user submits the Settings form, the `saveSettings()` function will run instead of the form actually getting submitted.

When the `saveSettings()` function is called, it grabs the values from the three form inputs using jQuery's `val()` function and saves each in a `localStorage` variable of the same name. Add this function to *kilo.js*:

```
function saveSettings() {
    localStorage.age = $('#age').val();
    localStorage.budget = $('#budget').val();
    localStorage.weight = $('#weight').val();
    jQT.goBack();
    return false;
}
```

Once the values are stored, I use the jQuery `goBack()` function (on the second to last line) to dismiss the panel and return to the previous page. I then return `false` to prevent the default action of the submit event that triggers this function. Had I omitted this line, the current page would reload, which is not what we want.

At this point, a user can launch the app, navigate to the Settings panel, enter her settings, and submit the form to save her settings to localStorage.

Since we are not clearing the fields when the form is submitted, the values that the user enters will still be there when she navigates back to the Settings panel. However, this is not because the values have been saved to localStorage; it's just because they are still just sitting there after having been typed in. Therefore, the next time the user launches that app and navigates to the Settings panel, the fields will be empty even though they have been saved.

To remedy this, we need to load the settings using the loadSettings() function, so add the following function to *kilo.js*:

```
function loadSettings() {
    $('#age').val(localStorage.age);
    $('#budget').val(localStorage.budget);
    $('#weight').val(localStorage.weight);
}
```

The loadSettings() function is the opposite of the saveSettings() function; i.e., it uses jQuery's val() function to set the three fields of the Settings form to the corresponding values saved in localStorage.

Now that we have a loadSettings() function, we need to trigger it. The most obvious time is probably when the app launches. To make this happen, I simply add a line to the document ready function in *kilo.js*:

```
$(document).ready(function(){
    $('#settings form').submit(saveSettings);
    loadSettings();
});
```

Unfortunately, loading the settings only at startup leaves a loophole that occurs if the user navigates to the Settings panel, changes some values, and taps the cancel button without submitting the form.

In this case, the newly changed values will still be sitting there the next time the user visits the Settings panel, even though the values were not saved. If the user closed and reopened the app, the displayed values would revert to the saved values because the loadSettings() function would refresh them at startup.

There are several ways that we could rectify this situation, but I think the most appropriate is to refresh the displayed values whenever the Settings panel begins to move, either into or out of view.

Thanks to jQTouch, this is a simple matter of binding the loadSettings() function to the pageAnimationStart event of the Settings panel. Replace the line you just added with the code shown in bold instead:

```
$(document).ready(function(){
    $('#settings form').submit(saveSettings);
    $('#settings').bind('pageAnimationStart', loadSettings);
});
```

The JavaScript contained in the *kilo.js* file now provides persistent data support for the Settings panel. When you view the code we've written to make this happen, there's really not much to it. Here is everything in *kilo.js* so far:

```
var jQT = $.jQTouch({
    icon: 'kilo.png',
    statusBar: 'black'
```

```
    });
    $(document).ready(function(){
        $('#settings form').submit(saveSettings);
        $('#settings').bind('pageAnimationStart', loadSettings);
    });
    function loadSettings() {
        $('#age').val(localStorage.age);
        $('#budget').val(localStorage.budget);
        $('#weight').val(localStorage.weight);
    }
    function saveSettings() {
        localStorage.age = $('#age').val();
        localStorage.budget = $('#budget').val();
        localStorage.weight = $('#weight').val();
        jQT.goBack();
        return false;
    }
```

Saving the Selected Date to sessionStorage

Ultimately, what I want to do is set up the Date panel such that when it's displayed, it will check the database for any records entered for that date, and display them as an edge-to-edge list. This requires that the Date panel know what date was tapped on the Dates panel.

I also want to allow the user to add and delete entries from the database, so I'll have to add support for the + button that already exists on the Date panel, and the Delete button in the Date panel entry template (more on this later).

The first step is to let the Date panel know what item was clicked in order to navigate to it from the Dates panel. With this piece of information, I can calculate the appropriate date context. To do this, I add some lines to the document ready function in *kilo.js*:

```
$(document).ready(function(){
    $('#settings form').submit(saveSettings);
    $('#settings').bind('pageAnimationStart', loadSettings);
    $('#dates li a').click(function(){❶
        var dayOffset = this.id;❷
        var date = new Date();❸
        date.setDate(date.getDate() - dayOffset);
        sessionStorage.currentDate = date.getMonth() + 1 + '/' +
                                     date.getDate() + '/' +
                                     date.getFullYear();❹
        refreshEntries();❺
    });
});
```

❶ On this line, I'm using jQuery's click() function to bind my own code to the click event of the links on the Dates panel.

❷ Here, I'm grabbing the id of the clicked object and storing it in the dayOffset variable. If you recall, the links on the Dates panel have ids ranging from 0 to 5, so the id of the clicked link will correspond to the number of days needed to calculate the clicked date (0 days in the past equals today, 1 day in the past equals yesterday, 2 days in the past equals the day before yesterday, etc.).

 In this context, the `this` keyword will contain a reference to the object that was the target of the click event.

❸ On this line, I create a new JavaScript date object and store it in a variable named `date`. Initially, this date will be pointed at the particular moment in time that it was created, so on the next line, I subtract the `dayOffset` from the result of the `getDate()` function, and then use `setDate()` to repoint the date.

❹ Here, I build a MM/DD/YYYY-formatted date string and save it to `sessionStorage` as `currentDate`.

 The `getMonth()` method of the date object returns values from 0–11, January being 0. Therefore, I have to add 1 to it to generate the correct value for the formatted string.

❺ Finally, I call the `refreshEntries()` function. The job of the `refreshEntries()` function is to update the incoming Date panel appropriately based on the date that was tapped on the Dates panel. For now, I'll just set it up to update the toolbar title of the Dates panel with the selected date, so you can see it's working. Without it, you'd just see the word "Date" as shown in Figure 5-1. Figure 5-2 shows the `refreshEntries()` function in action.

Here's the code for the `refreshEntries()` function:

```
function refreshEntries() {
    var currentDate = sessionStorage.currentDate;
    $('#date h1').text(currentDate);
}
```

Next, we'll move on to a more powerful and complex client-side data storage method that we'll use to store the user's food entries on the Date panel.

Client-Side Database

Of all the exciting features of HTML5, the one that rocks my world the most is client-side database support. It allows developers to use a simple but powerful JavaScript database API to store persistent data in a relational format.

Developers can use standard SQL statements to create tables; to insert, update, select, and delete rows; and so on. The JavaScript database API even supports transactions.

Figure 5-1. Before the refreshEntries() function, the title just says "Date"

Figure 5-2. After the refreshEntries() function, the title reflects the selected date

We're talking about SQL here, so there is an inherent complexity. Regardless, this is a game-changing feature, so time spent getting your head around it will be well rewarded.

Creating a Database

Now that our Date panel knows what date the user has selected, we have all the info we need to allow users to create entries. Before we can write the `createEntry` function, we need to set up a database table to store the submitted data. I'll add some lines to *kilo.js* to do so:

```
var db;❶
$(document).ready(function(){
    $('#settings form').submit(saveSettings);
    $('#settings').bind('pageAnimationStart', loadSettings);
    $('#dates li a').click(function(){
        var dayOffset = this.id;
        var date = new Date();
        date.setDate(date.getDate() - dayOffset);
        sessionStorage.currentDate = date.getMonth() + 1 + '/' +
                                     date.getDate() + '/' +
                                     date.getFullYear();

        refreshEntries();
    });
    var shortName = 'Kilo';❷
    var version = '1.0';
    var displayName = 'Kilo';
    var maxSize = 65536;
    db = openDatabase(shortName, version, displayName, maxSize);❸
    db.transaction(❹
        function(transaction) {❺
            transaction.executeSql(❻
                'CREATE TABLE IF NOT EXISTS entries ' +
                ' (id INTEGER NOT NULL PRIMARY KEY AUTOINCREMENT, ' +
                '  date DATE NOT NULL, food TEXT NOT NULL, ' +
                ' calories INTEGER NOT NULL );'
            );
        }
    );
});
```

❶ The first thing to note is that I've added a variable named `db` to the global scope of the application. This variable will be used to hold a reference to the database connection once we've established it. I defined it in the global scope because we're going to have to refer to it all over the place.

❷ On these four lines, I'm defining some `var`s for the `openDatabase` call:

shortName
>   A string that will be used to refer to the database file on disk.

version
>   A number that you can use to manage upgrades and backward compatibility when you need to change your database schema.

displayName
>   A string that will be presented to the user in the interface. For example, the display name appears in the Settings application on the iPhone in the Settings→Safari→Databases panel.

maxSize
>   The maximum number of kilobytes to which you think your database will grow.

Database size limits are still being implemented by browser vendors at this time, so some trial and error while testing your application is in order. The current default on the iPhone is 5 MB. If your database grows beyond this limit, the user will automatically be asked to allow or deny the size increase. If he allows the increase, the database size limit will be upped to 10 MB. If he denies the increase, a QUOTA_ERR error will be returned. See Table 5-1 for a list of database error codes.

❸ With my parameters set, I call openDatabase on this line and store the connection in the db variable. If the database doesn't already exist, it will be created.

Now that we have a database connection, we need to create an entries table if one doesn't already exist.

❹ All database queries must take place in the context of a transaction, so I begin one here by calling the transaction method of the db object. The remaining lines comprise a function that is sent to the transaction as the sole parameter.

❺ Here, I begin an anonymous function and pass the transaction into it. To be perfectly honest, passing the transaction into its own callback function makes no sense to me, but that's what you have to do.

❻ Once inside the function, I call the executeSql method of the transaction object to execute a standard CREATE TABLE query.

If you were to launch the app as is, it would create a database named Kilo on your iPhone. You can see this by navigating to Settings→Safari→Databases→Kilo on the iPhone. Figure 5-3 shows the database settings.

Figure 5-3. The database panel on the iPhone

In the desktop version of Safari, you can actually view and interact with your client-side databases by navigating to Develop→Show Web Inspector, then clicking the Databases tab. (If the Develop menu is not available, go into Safari's Preferences and enable the Develop menu on the Advanced preferences page.)

 The Databases tab is named Storage in WebKit. I think Storage is a more accurate name, so I wouldn't be surprised if this change eventually shows up in Safari.

The Web Inspector included in desktop Safari is extremely helpful when debugging. By default, it appears as a pane of your current browser window. If you click the undock icon (hover over the icons at the bottom left to see what they do), Web Inspector will appear in a separate window as shown in Figure 5-4. The interface even allows you to send arbitrary SQL queries to the database by clicking on the database name (see Figure 5-5).

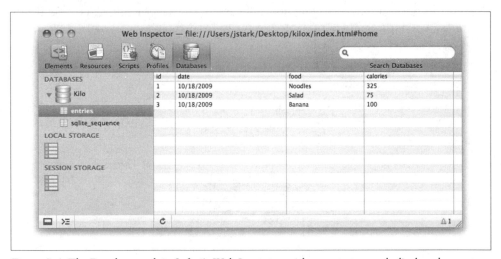

Figure 5-4. The Databases tab in Safari's Web Inspector with some test records displayed

Inserting Rows

Now that we have a database set up to receive some entries, we can start building the createEntry() function. First, you have to override the submit event of the #createEntry form. You can do so by binding the createEntry() function to the submit event in the document ready function in *kilo.js* (here I just show the first few lines, with the added line of code in bold):

```
$(document).ready(function(){
    $('#createEntry form').submit(createEntry);
    $('#settings form').submit(saveSettings);
```

```
$('#settings').bind('pageAnimationStart', loadSettings);
...
```

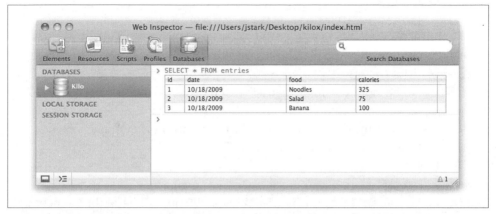

Figure 5-5. The Databases tab in Safari's Web Inspector allows you to execute arbitrary SQL statements against your database

Now when a user submits the #createEntry form, the createEntry() function will be called. Next, add the following to *kilo.js* to create the record in the database:

```
function createEntry() {
    var date = sessionStorage.currentDate;❶
    var calories = $('#calories').val();
    var food = $('#food').val();
    db.transaction(❷
        function(transaction) {
            transaction.executeSql(
                'INSERT INTO entries (date, calories, food) VALUES (?, ?, ?);',
                [date, calories, food],
                function(){
                    refreshEntries();
                    jQT.goBack();
                },
                errorHandler
            );
        }
    );
    return false;
}
```

❶ I'm setting some variables that I'm going to use in the SQL query. If you recall, the date that the user tapped on the Dates panel will be stored in sessionStorage.currentDate. The other two values (calories and food) are pulled out of the data entry form using the same approach that we saw earlier with the Settings form.

❷ Then, I open a database transaction and run an executeSql() call. Here I am passing four parameters to the executeSql() method:

```
'INSERT INTO entries (date, calories, food) VALUES (?, ?, ?);'
```
> This is the statement that will be executed. The question marks are data placeholders.

```
[date, calories, food]
```
> This is an array of the values being sent to the database. They correspond by position with the data placeholder question marks in the SQL statement.

```
function(){refreshEntries();jQT.goBack();}
```
> This anonymous function will execute if the SQL query is successful.

```
errorHandler
```
> This is the name of the function that will execute if the SQL query fails.

Error handling

Assuming the insert is successful, the anonymous function passed as the third parameter will be executed. It calls the `refreshEntries()` function (which at the moment only updates the title of the Date panel, but will soon cause the entries you create to appear in the list there), and it calls jQTouch's `goBack()` function to dismiss the New Entry panel and return to the Date panel.

If the insert is not successful, the `errorHandler()` function will run. Add the following to the *kilo.js* file:

```
function errorHandler(transaction, error) {
    alert('Oops. Error was '+error.message+' (Code '+error.code+')');
    return true;
}
```

The error handler is passed two parameters: the transaction object and the error object. Here, I'm using the error object to alert the user to the message and error code that were thrown.

Error handlers must return true or false. When an error handler returns true (i.e., "Yes, this is a fatal error"), execution is halted and the entire transaction is rolled back. When an error handler returns false (i.e., "No, this is not a fatal error"), execution will continue.

In some cases, you might want to branch based on the type of error to decide whether you should return true or false. Table 5-1 shows the current possible error codes according to the W3C Web Database working draft specification.

Table 5-1. Web database error codes

Constant	Code	Situation
UNKNOWN_ERR	0	The transaction failed for reasons unrelated to the database itself and not covered by any other error code.
DATABASE_ERR	1	The statement failed for database reasons not covered by any other error code.

Constant	Code	Situation
VERSION_ERR	2	The operation failed because the actual database version was not what it should be. For example, a statement found that the actual database version no longer matched the expected version of the Database or DatabaseSync object, or the Database.changeVersion() or DatabaseSync.changeVersion() method was passed a version that doesn't match the actual database version.
TOO_LARGE_ERR	3	The statement failed because the data returned from the database was too large. The SQL LIMIT modifier might be useful to reduce the size of the result set.
QUOTA_ERR	4	The statement failed because there was not enough remaining storage space, or the storage quota was reached and the user declined to give more space to the database.
SYNTAX_ERR	5	The statement failed because of a syntax error, or the number of arguments did not match the number of ? placeholders in the statement, or the statement tried to use a statement that is not allowed, such as BEGIN, COMMIT, or ROLLBACK, or the statement tried to use a verb that could modify the database but the transaction was read-only.
CONSTRAINT_ERR	6	An INSERT, UPDATE, or REPLACE statement failed due to a constraint failure. For example, a row was being inserted and the value given for the primary key column duplicated the value of an existing row.
TIMEOUT_ERR	7	A lock for the transaction could not be obtained in a reasonable time.

You may have noticed that the error handler function accepts a transaction object in addition to the error object. It's conceivable that in some cases you might want to execute a SQL statement inside of the error handler, perhaps to log the error or record some metadata for debugging or crash reporting purposes. The transaction object parameter allows you to make more **executeSql()** calls from inside the error handler, like so:

```
function errorHandler(transaction, error) {
  alert('Oops. Error was '+error.message+' (Code '+error.code+')');
  transaction.executeSql('INSERT INTO errors (code, message) VALUES (?, ?);',
                         [error.code, error.message]);
  return false;
}
```

Please take special note of the fact that I have to return **false** from the error handler if I want my **executeSql()** statement to run. If I return **true** (or nothing at all), the entire transaction—including this SQL statement—will be rolled back, thereby preventing the desired result.

Transaction Callback Handlers

Although I won't be doing so in my examples, you should know that you can also specify success and error handlers on the **transaction** method itself. This gives you a convenient location to execute code after a long series of **executeSql()** statements have been completed.

Oddly, the parameter order for the `transaction` method's callbacks is defined to be error, then success (the reverse of the order for `executeSql()`). Here's a version of the `createEntry()` function with transaction callbacks added toward the end:

```
function createEntry() {
    var date = sessionStorage.currentDate;
    var calories = $('#calories').val();
    var food = $('#food').val();
    db.transaction(
        function(transaction) {
            transaction.executeSql(
                'INSERT INTO entries (date, calories, food) VALUES (?, ?, ?);',
                [date, calories, food],
                function(){
                    refreshEntries();
                    jQT.goBack();
                },
                errorHandler
            );
        },
        transactionErrorHandler,
        transactionSuccessHandler
    );
    return false;
}
```

Selecting Rows and Handling Result Sets

The next step is to expand the `refreshEntries()` function to do more than just set the title bar to the selected date. Specifically, I'm going to query the database for entries on the selected date, and then append them to the `#date ul` element using the hidden `entryTemplate` HTML for structure. It's been a while since we looked at that code, so here's the Date panel again:

```
<div id="date">
    <div class="toolbar">
        <h1>Date</h1>
        <a class="button back" href="#">Back</a>
        <a class="button slideup" href="#createEntry">+</a>
    </div>
    <ul class="edgetoedge">
        <li id="entryTemplate" class="entry" style="display:none">❶
            <span class="label">Label</span>
            <span class="calories">000</span>
            <span class="delete">Delete</span>
        </li>
    </ul>
</div>
```

❶ Recall that I had set the style attribute of the `li` to `display: none`, which causes it not to show up on the page. I did this so I could use that HTML snippet as a template for the database rows.

Here's the complete refreshEntries() function, which you must use to replace the existing refreshEntries() function:

```
function refreshEntries() {
    var currentDate = sessionStorage.currentDate;❶
    $('#date h1').text(currentDate);
    $('#date ul li:gt(0)').remove();❷
    db.transaction(❸
        function(transaction) {
            transaction.executeSql(
                'SELECT * FROM entries WHERE date = ? ORDER BY food;',❹
                [currentDate], ❺
                function (transaction, result) {❻
                    for (var i=0; i < result.rows.length; i++) {
                        var row = result.rows.item(i);❼
                        var newEntryRow = $('#entryTemplate').clone();❽
                        newEntryRow.removeAttr('id');
                        newEntryRow.removeAttr('style');
                        newEntryRow.data('entryId', row.id);❾
                        newEntryRow.appendTo('#date ul');❿
                        newEntryRow.find('.label').text(row.food);
                        newEntryRow.find('.calories').text(row.calories);
                    }
                },
                errorHandler
            );
        }
    );
}
```

❶ These two lines set the toolbar title of the Date panel to the contents of the currentDate value saved in sessionStorage.

❷ On this line I'm using jQuery's gt() function (gt stands for "greater than") to select and remove any li elements with an index greater than 0. The first time through, this will do nothing because the only li will be the one with the id of entryTemplate, which has an index of 0. However, on subsequent visits to the page we need to remove any additional lis before appending rows from the database again. Otherwise, items would end up appearing multiple times in the list.

❸ On these three lines, I'm setting up a database transaction and the executeSql statement.

❹ This line contains the first parameter for the executeSql statement. It's a simple SELECT statement with a question mark acting as a data placeholder.

❺ This is a single-element array that contains the currently selected date. This will replace the question mark in the SQL query. Note that quotes around the ? are not necessary—escaping and quoting of data is handled automatically.

❻ This anonymous function will be called in the event of a successful query. It accepts two parameters: transaction and result.

The transaction object can be used within the success handler to send new queries to the database, as we saw with the error handler previously. However, there is no need to do that in this case, so we won't be using it.

The result object is what we are most interested in here. It has three read-only properties: rowsAffected, which you can use to determine the number of rows affected by an insert, update, or delete query; insertId, which returns the primary key of the last row created in an insert operation; and rows, which has the found records.

The rows object will contain 0 or more row objects, and also has a length property that I use in the for loop on the next line.

❼ On this line, I use the item() method of the rows object to set the row variable to the contents of the current row.

❽ On this line, I clone() the template li and remove its id and style attributes on the next two lines. Removing the style will make the row visible, and removing the id is important because otherwise we would end up with multiple items on the page with the same id.

❾ On this line, I store the value of the row's id property as data on the li itself (we'll need that later if the user decides to delete the entry).

❿ This is where I append the li element to the parent ul. On the next two lines, I update the label and calories span child elements of the li with the corresponding data from the row object.

With all this out of the way, our Date panel will display an li for each row in the database that corresponds to the selected date. Each row will have a label, calories, and a Delete button. Once we create a few rows, you can see that we need to add a bit of CSS to style things up nicely (Figure 5-6).

Save the following CSS into a file named *kilo.css*:

```
#date ul li {
    position: relative;
}
#date ul li span {
    color: #FFFFFF;
    text-shadow: rgba(0,0,0,.7) 0 1px 2px;
}
#date ul li .delete {
    position: absolute;
    top: 5px;
    right: 6px;
    font-size: 12px;
    line-height: 30px;
    padding: 0 3px;
    border-width: 0 5px;
    -webkit-border-image: url(themes/jqt/img/button.png) 0 5 0 5;
}
```

Now, link to *kilo.css* by adding the following line to the head section of *index.html*:

```
<link type="text/css" rel="stylesheet" media="screen" href="kilo.css">
```

Figure 5-6. The entries are showing up now, but they need to be fancied up with some CSS

Although the Delete buttons now look like buttons, they won't do anything when tapped at this point (see Figure 5-7). This is because I set them up using the span tag, which is not an interactive element in an HTML page.

Figure 5-7. The entries with CSS applied

Deleting Rows

To make my Delete buttons do something when clicked, I need to bind a click event handler to them with jQuery. I did the same sort of thing earlier with the items on the Date panel using jQuery's `click()` method.

Unfortunately, that approach won't work in this case. Unlike the items on the Dates panel, the entries on the Date panel are not static—they are added and removed throughout the course of the user's session. In fact, when the application launches, there are no entries visible on the Date panel at all. Therefore, we have nothing to bind the click to at launch.

The solution is to bind click events to the Delete buttons as they are created by the `refreshEntries()` function. To do so, add the following to the end of the `for` loop:

```
newEntryRow.find('.delete').click(function(){❶
    var clickedEntry = $(this).parent();❷
    var clickedEntryId = clickedEntry.data('entryId');❸
    deleteEntryById(clickedEntryId);❹
    clickedEntry.slideUp();
});
```

❶ The function begins by specifying that we are looking for any elements that match the `#date .delete` selector, and calling the `click()` method on those elements. The `click()` method accepts the anonymous function that will be used to handle the event as its only parameter.

❷ When the click handler is triggered, the parent of the Delete button (i.e., the `li`) is located and stored in the `clickedEntry` variable.

❸ On this line, I'm setting the `clickedEntryId` variable to the value of the `entryId` I stored on the `li` element when it was created by the `refreshEntries()` function.

❹ On this line, I pass the clicked `id` into the `deleteEntryById()` function, and then on the next line, I use jQuery's `slideUp()` method to gracefully remove the `li` from the page.

JavaScript gurus in the crowd might wonder why I didn't use jQuery's `live()` function to bind the delete handler to the Delete buttons. Unfortunately, the `live()` function doesn't work with `click` on the iPhone because `click` isn't the event that bubbles up the DOM. For more information on jQuery's `live()` function, please visit *http://docs.jquery.com/Events/live#typefn*.

Add the following `deleteEntryById()` function to *kilo.js* to remove the entry from the database:

```
function deleteEntryById(id) {
    db.transaction(
        function(transaction) {
```

```
        transaction.executeSql('DELETE FROM entries WHERE id=?;',
            [id], null, errorHandler);
    }
    );
}
```

As we've seen in previous examples, I open a transaction, pass it a callback function with the transaction object as the parameter, and call the `executeSql()` method. I'm passing in the SQL query and the `id` of the clicked record as the first two arguments. The third argument is where the success handler would go, but I don't need one, so I just specify `null`. As the fourth argument, I specify the same default error handler that we've been using all along.

And there you have it. It may have taken a lot of description to get to this point, but in reality we haven't had to write all that much code. In fact, the completed *kilo.js* file (Example 5-1) only contains 108 lines of JavaScript.

Example 5-1. The complete JavaScript listing for Kilo database interaction

```
var jQT = $.jQTouch({
    icon: 'kilo.png',
    statusBar: 'black'
});
var db;
$(document).ready(function(){
    $('#createEntry form').submit(createEntry);
    $('#settings form').submit(saveSettings);
    $('#settings').bind('pageAnimationStart', loadSettings);
    $('#dates li a').click(function(){
        var dayOffset = this.id;
        var date = new Date();
        date.setDate(date.getDate() - dayOffset);
        sessionStorage.currentDate = date.getMonth() + 1 + '/' +
                                     date.getDate() + '/' +
                                     date.getFullYear();
        refreshEntries();
    });
    var shortName = 'Kilo';
    var version = '1.0';
    var displayName = 'Kilo';
    var maxSize = 65536;
    db = openDatabase(shortName, version, displayName, maxSize);
    db.transaction(
        function(transaction) {
            transaction.executeSql(
                'CREATE TABLE IF NOT EXISTS entries ' +
                '    (id INTEGER NOT NULL PRIMARY KEY AUTOINCREMENT, ' +
                '    date DATE NOT NULL, food TEXT NOT NULL, ' +
                '    calories INTEGER NOT NULL);'
            );
        }
    );
});
function loadSettings() {
```

```
        $('#age').val(localStorage.age);
        $('#budget').val(localStorage.budget);
        $('#weight').val(localStorage.weight);
}
function saveSettings() {
        localStorage.age = $('#age').val();
        localStorage.budget = $('#budget').val();
        localStorage.weight = $('#weight').val();
        jQT.goBack();
        return false;
}
function createEntry() {
        var date = sessionStorage.currentDate;
        var calories = $('#calories').val();
        var food = $('#food').val();
        db.transaction(
            function(transaction) {
                transaction.executeSql(
                    'INSERT INTO entries (date, calories, food) VALUES (?, ?, ?);',
                    [date, calories, food],
                    function(){
                        refreshEntries();
                        jQT.goBack();
                    },
                    errorHandler
                );
            }
        );
        return false;
}
function refreshEntries() {
        var currentDate = sessionStorage.currentDate;
        $('#date h1').text(currentDate);
        $('#date ul li:gt(0)').remove();
        db.transaction(
            function(transaction) {
                transaction.executeSql(
                    'SELECT * FROM entries WHERE date = ? ORDER BY food;',
                    [currentDate],
                    function (transaction, result) {
                        for (var i=0; i < result.rows.length; i++) {
                            var row = result.rows.item(i);
                            var newEntryRow = $('#entryTemplate').clone();
                            newEntryRow.removeAttr('id');
                            newEntryRow.removeAttr('style');
                            newEntryRow.data('entryId', row.id);
                            newEntryRow.appendTo('#date ul');
                            newEntryRow.find('.label').text(row.food);
                            newEntryRow.find('.calories').text(row.calories);
                            newEntryRow.find('.delete').click(function(){
                                var clickedEntry = $(this).parent();
                                var clickedEntryId = clickedEntry.data('entryId');
                                deleteEntryById(clickedEntryId);
                                clickedEntry.slideUp();
                            });
```

```
                }
            },
            errorHandler
        );
        }
    );
}
function deleteEntryById(id) {
    db.transaction(
        function(transaction) {
            transaction.executeSql('DELETE FROM entries WHERE id=?;',
                [id], null, errorHandler);
        }
    );
}
function errorHandler(transaction, error) {
    alert('Oops. Error was '+error.message+' (Code '+error.code+')');
    return true;
}
```

What You've Learned

In this chapter, you learned two ways to store user data on the client: key/value storage, and the client-side SQL database. The client-side database in particular opens up a world of possibilities for web-based application developers.

The only thing stopping us from running this example application in offline mode is that we have to initially connect to the web server each time the app is launched to download the HTML and related resources. Wouldn't it be *schweet* if we could just cache all that stuff locally on the device?

Yeah, it would. On to the next chapter!

CHAPTER 6

Going Offline

There's a feature of HTML5 called the *offline application cache* that allows users to run web apps even when they are not connected to the Internet. It works like this: when a user navigates to your web app, the browser downloads and stores all the files it needs to display the page (HTML, CSS, JavaScript, images, etc.). The next time the user navigates to your web app, the browser will recognize the URL and serve the files out of the local application cache instead of pulling them across the network.

The Basics of the Offline Application Cache

The main component of the offline application cache is a *cache manifest file* that you host on your web server. I'm going to use a simple example to explain the concepts involved, and then I'll show you how to apply what you've learned to the Kilo example we've been working on.

A manifest file is just a simple text document that lives on your web server and is sent to the user's device with a content type of `cache-manifest`. The manifest contains a list of files that a user's device must download and save in order to function. Consider a web directory containing the following files:

```
index.html
logo.jpg
scripts/demo.js
styles/screen.css
```

In this case, `index.html` is the page that will load into the browser when users visit your application. The other files are referenced from within `index.html`. To make everything available offline, create a file named `demo.manifest` in the directory with `index.html`. Here's a directory listing showing the added file:

```
demo.manifest
index.html
logo.jpg
scripts/demo.js
styles/screen.css
```

Next, add the following lines to `demo.manifest`:

```
CACHE MANIFEST
index.html
logo.jpg
scripts/demo.js
styles/screen.css
```

The paths in the manifest are relative to the location of the manifest file. You can also use absolute URLs, like so:

```
CACHE MANIFEST
http://www.example.com/index.html
http://www.example.com/logo.jpg
http://www.example.com/scripts/demo.js
http://www.example.com/styles/screen.css
```

Now that the manifest file is created, you need to link to it by adding a manifest attribute to the HTML tag inside `index.html`:

```
<html manifest="demo.manifest">
```

You must serve the manifest file with the `text/cache-manifest` content type or the browser will not recognize it. If you are using the Apache web server or a compatible web server, you can accomplish this by adding an *.htaccess* file to your web directory with the following line:

```
AddType text/cache-manifest .manifest
```

> If the *.htaccess* file doesn't work for you, refer to the portion of your web server documentation that pertains to *MIME types*. You must associate the file extension *.manifest* with the MIME type of `text/cache-manifest`. If your website is hosted by a web hosting provider, your provider may have a control panel for your website where you can add the appropriate MIME type. I'll also show you an example that uses a PHP script in place of the *.htaccess* file a little later on in this chapter.

Mac OS X and the .htaccess File

If you are serving up web pages on your local network using the Apache web server that's included with Mac OS X, it will ignore any *.htaccess* file in your personal web folder (the *Sites* folder that's in your home directory). However, you can enable support for *.htaccess* by opening Applications→Utilities→Terminal and typing these commands (you'll need to type your password when prompted):

```
cd /etc/apache2/users
sudo pico $USER.conf
```

This loads your personal Apache configuration file into the Pico editor. (You can see a list of editor commands at the bottom of the screen; the ^ symbol indicates the Control key.) Use the arrow keys to move down to the line `AllowOverride None`, and replace the

---

word None with the word All. Then press Control-X to exit, answer Y to save changes, and press Return to save the file. Then, start System Preferences, go to Sharing, and, if needed, click the lock icon labeled "Click the lock to make changes" and type your password when prompted. Finally, clear the checkbox next to Web Sharing and then check it again (this restarts Web Sharing). The web server on your Mac should now respect the settings in any .htaccess files you put in your Sites directory or its subdirectories.

Our offline application cache is now in working order. The next time a user browses to *http://example.com/index.html*, the page and its resources will load normally over the network. In the background, all the files listed in the manifest will be downloaded to the user's local disk (or her iPhone's flash memory). Once the download completes and the user refreshes the page, she'll be accessing the local files only. She can now disconnect from the Internet and continue to access the web app.

So now that the user is accessing our files locally on her device, we have a new problem: how does she get updates when changes are made to the website?

When the user does have access to the Internet and navigates to the URL of our web app, her browser checks the manifest file on our site to see if it still matches the local copy. If the remote manifest has changed, the browser downloads all the files listed in it. It downloads these in the background to a temporary cache.

 The comparison between the local manifest and the remote manifest is a byte-by-byte comparison of the file contents (including comments and blank lines). The file modification timestamp and changes to any of the resources themselves are irrelevant when determining whether or not changes have been made.

If something goes wrong during the download (e.g., the user loses her Internet connection), then the partially downloaded cache is automatically discarded and the previous one remains in effect. If the download is successful, the new local files will be used the next time the user launches the app.

Application Cache Download Behavior

Remember that when a manifest is updated, the download of the new files takes place in the background *after* the initial launch of the app. This means that even after the download completes, the user will still be working with the old files. In other words, the currently loaded page and all of its related files don't automagically reload when the download completes. The new files that were downloaded in the background will not become visible until the user relaunches the app.

> This is very similar to standard desktop app update behavior. You launch an app; it tells you that updates are available; you click to download updates; the download completes; and you are prompted to relaunch the app for the updates to take effect.

Online Whitelist and Fallback Options

It is possible to force the browser to always access certain resources over the network. This means that the browser will not cache those resources locally, and that they will not be available when the user is offline. To specify a resource as online only, you use the `NETWORK:` keyword (the trailing : is essential) in the manifest file like so:

```
CACHE MANIFEST
index.html
scripts/demo.js
styles/screen.css

NETWORK:
logo.jpg
```

Here, I've whitelisted *logo.jpg* by moving it into the `NETWORK` section of the manifest file. When the user is offline, the image will show up as a broken image link (Figure 6-1). When he is online, it will appear normally (Figure 6-2).

Figure 6-1. Whitelisted images will show up as broken links when the user is offline

If you don't want offline users to see the broken image, you can use the FALLBACK keyword to specify a fallback resource like so:

```
CACHE MANIFEST
index.html
scripts/demo.js
styles/screen.css

FALLBACK:
logo.jpg offline.jpg
```

Figure 6-2. Whitelisted images will show up normally when the user is online

Now, when the user is offline, he'll see *offline.jpg* (Figure 6-3), and when he's online he'll see *logo.jpg* (Figure 6-4).

This becomes even more useful when you consider that you can specify a single fallback image for multiple resources by using a partial path. Let's say I add an *images* directory to my website and put some files in it:

```
/demo.manifest
/index.html
/images/logo.jpg
/images/logo2.jpg
/images/offline.jpg
/scripts/demo.js
/styles/screen.css
```

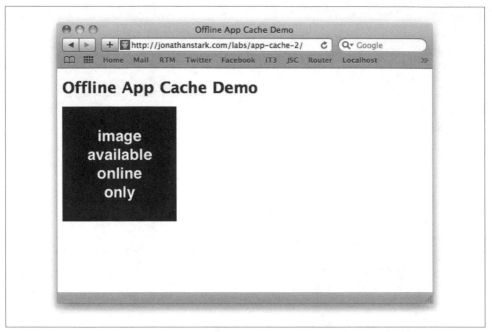

Figure 6-3. Fallback images will show up when the user is offline

Figure 6-4. Hosted images will show up normally when the user is online

I can now tell the browser to fall back to *offline.jpg* for anything contained in the *images* directory like so:

```
CACHE MANIFEST
index.html
scripts/demo.js
styles/screen.css

FALLBACK:
images/ images/offline.jpg
```

Now, when the user is offline, he'll see *offline.jpg* (Figure 6-5), and when he's online he'll see *logo.jpg* and *logo2.jpg* (Figure 6-6).

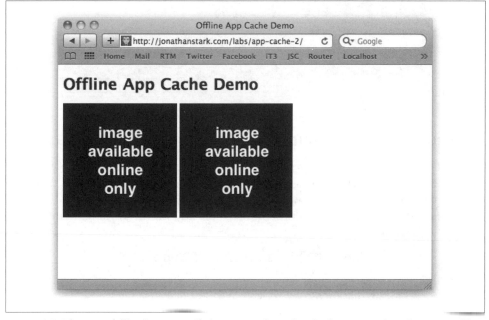

Figure 6-5. The same fallback image will show up in place of multiple images when the user is offline

Whether you should add resources to the NETWORK or FALLBACK section of the manifest file depends on the nature of your application. Keep in mind that the offline application cache is primarily intended to store apps locally on a device. It's not really meant to be used to decrease server load, increase performance, and so on.

In most cases you should be listing all of the files required to run your app in the manifest file. If you have a lot of dynamic content and you are not sure how to reference it in the manifest, your app is probably not a good fit for the offline application cache and you might want to consider a different approach (a client-side database, perhaps).

Figure 6-6. Hosted images will show up normally when the user is online

Creating a Dynamic Manifest File

Now that we're comfortable with how the offline app cache works, let's apply it to the Kilo example we've been working on. Kilo consists of quite a few files, and manually listing them all in a manifest file would be a pain. Moreover, a single typo would invalidate the entire manifest file and prevent the application from working offline.

Running PHP Scripts on Your Web Server

PHP is a versatile web scripting language and is supported by most web hosting providers. This means that on most web servers, you can create a file whose name ends with the extension *.php*, add some PHP code to it, visit it in your web browser, and it will just work. If you've been using a web server on your personal computer to serve up pages to your iPhone, you'll need to get set up to run PHP scripts. If you're running a web server on Windows, see *http://php.net/manual/en/install.windows.php* for downloads and information. PHP is easy to install on Linux (for example, Ubuntu users can simply type `sudo aptitude install apache2 php5` at a shell prompt).

Macs come with PHP installed, but you need to take a step to enable it. Similar to what you did in "Mac OS X and the .htaccess File" on page 92, open Applications→Utilities→Terminal and type these commands (you'll need to type your password when prompted):

```
cd /etc/apache2
sudo pico httpd.conf
```

Next, press Control-W. This brings up the option to search the file. Type "php5" and then press Return. This brings you to a line that should look like this:

```
#LoadModule php5_module        libexec/apache2/libphp5.so
```

Using the arrow keys, move to the beginning of the line and delete the # comment character, which is preventing this line from having any effect. Then press Control-X to exit, answer Y to save changes, and then press Return to save the file. Next, start System Preferences, go to Sharing, and, if needed, click the lock icon labeled "Click the lock to make changes" and type your password when prompted. Then, clear the checkbox next to Web Sharing and check it again. Now PHP should be enabled on your Mac's web server.

Next, create a file in the *Sites* subdirectory of your home folder named *test.php* with these contents:

```
<?php
  phpinfo();
?>
```

Finally, visit the following URL in your browser: `http://localhost/~YOURUSERNAME/test.php`. Replace YOURUSERNAME with your username, but don't delete the ~. (You can find out your username at the Terminal by typing `echo $USER` and pressing Return.) If PHP is working, you'll see a table displaying your PHP version number and a lot of other information about your PHP installation. If it is not working, you'll see nothing but a blank page. Visit *http://www.php.net/support.php* for links to sources of documentation and help with using PHP.

To address this issue, we're going to write a little PHP file that reads the contents of the application directory (and its subdirectories) and creates the file list for us. Create a new file in your Kilo directory named *manifest.php* and add the following code:

```
<?php
  header('Content-Type: text/cache-manifest');❶
  echo "CACHE MANIFEST\n";❷

  $dir = new RecursiveDirectoryIterator(".");❸
  foreach(new RecursiveIteratorIterator($dir) as $file) {❹
    if ($file->IsFile() &&❺
        $file != "./manifest.php" &&
        substr($file->getFilename(), 0, 1) != ".")
    {
      echo $file . "\n";❻
    }
  }
?>
```

❶ I'm using the PHP `header` function to output this file with the `cache-manifest` content type. Doing this is an alternative to using an *.htaccess* file to specify the content type for the manifest file. In fact, you can remove the *.htaccess* file you created in "The Basics of the Offline Application Cache" on page 92, if you are not using it for any other purpose.

❷ As you saw earlier in this chapter, the first line of a cache manifest file must be CACHE MANIFEST. As far as the browser is concerned, this is the first line of the document; the PHP file runs on the web server, and the browser only sees the output of commands that emit text, such as echo.

❸ This line creates an object called $dir, which enumerates all the files in the current directory. It does so recursively, which means that if you have any files in subdirectories, it will find them, too.

❹ Each time the program passes through this loop, it sets the variable $file to an object that represents one of the files in the current directory. In English, this line would read: "Each time through, set the file variable to the next file found in the current directory or its subdirectories."

❺ The if statement here checks to make sure that the file is actually a file (and not a directory or symbolic link). It also ignores files named *manifest.php* or any file that starts with a . (such as *.htaccess*).

 The leading ./ is part of the file's full path; the . refers to the current directory and the / separates elements of the file's path. So there's always a ./ that appears before the filename in the output. However, when I check for a leading . in the filename I use the getFilename function, which returns the filename without the leading path. This way, I can detect files beginning with . even if they are buried in a subdirectory.

❻ Here's where I display each file's name.

To the browser, *manifest.php* will look like this:

```
CACHE MANIFEST
./index.html
./jqtouch/jqtouch.css
./jqtouch/jqtouch.js
./jqtouch/jqtouch.transitions.js
./jqtouch/jquery.js
./kilo.css
./kilo.js
./themes/apple/img/backButton.png
./themes/apple/img/blueButton.png
./themes/apple/img/cancel.png
./themes/apple/img/chevron.png
./themes/apple/img/grayButton.png
./themes/apple/img/listArrowSel.png
./themes/apple/img/listGroup.png
./themes/apple/img/loading.gif
./themes/apple/img/on_off.png
./themes/apple/img/pinstripes.png
./themes/apple/img/selection.png
./themes/apple/img/thumb.png
./themes/apple/img/toggle.png
./themes/apple/img/toggleOn.png
```

```
./themes/apple/img/toolbar.png
./themes/apple/img/toolButton.png
./themes/apple/img/whiteButton.png
./themes/apple/theme.css
./themes/jqt/img/back_button.png
./themes/jqt/img/back_button_clicked.png
./themes/jqt/img/button.png
./themes/jqt/img/button_clicked.png
./themes/jqt/img/chevron.png
./themes/jqt/img/chevron_circle.png
./themes/jqt/img/grayButton.png
./themes/jqt/img/loading.gif
./themes/jqt/img/on_off.png
./themes/jqt/img/rowhead.png
./themes/jqt/img/toggle.png
./themes/jqt/img/toggleOn.png
./themes/jqt/img/toolbar.png
./themes/jqt/img/whiteButton.png
./themes/jqt/theme.css
```

 Try loading the page yourself in a browser (be sure to load it with an HTTP URL such as `http://localhost/~YOURUSERNAME/manifest.php`). If you see a lot more files in your listing, you may have some extraneous files from the jQTouch distribution. The files *LICENSE.txt*, *README.txt*, and *sample.htaccess* are safe to delete, as are the directories *demos* and *extensions*. If you see a number of directories named *.svn*, you may also safely delete them, though they will not be visible in the Mac OS X Finder (you can work with them from within the Terminal, however).

Now open *index.html* and add a reference *manifest.php* like so:

```
<html manifest="manifest.php">
```

Now that the manifest is generated dynamically, let's modify it so that its contents change when any of the files in the directory change (remember that the client will redownload the application only if the manifest's contents have changed). Here is the modified *manifest.php*:

```
<?php
  header('Content-Type: text/cache-manifest');
  echo "CACHE MANIFEST\n";

  $hashes = "";①

  $dir = new RecursiveDirectoryIterator(".");
  foreach(new RecursiveIteratorIterator($dir) as $file) {
    if ($file->IsFile() &&
        $file != "./manifest.php" &&
        substr($file->getFilename(), 0, 1) != ".")
    {
      echo $file . "\n";
```

```
        $hashes .= md5_file($file); ❷
    }
}
echo "# Hash: " . md5($hashes) . "\n"; ❸
?>
```

❶ Here, I'm initializing a string that will hold the *hashed* values of the files.

❷ On this line I'm computing the hash of each file using PHP's `md5_file` function (Message-Digest algorithm 5), and appending it to the end of the `$hashes` string. Any change to the file, however small, will also change the results of the `md5_file` function. The hash is a 32-character string, such as "4ac3c9c004cac7785fa6b132b4f18efc".

❸ Here's where I take the big string of hashes (all of the 32-character strings for each file concatenated together), and compute an MD5 hash of the string itself. This gives us a short (32 characters, instead of 32 multiplied by the number of files) string that's printed out as a comment (beginning with the comment symbol #).

From the viewpoint of the client browser, there's nothing special about this line. It's a comment, and the client browser ignores it. However, if one of the files is modified, this line will change, which means the manifest has changed.

Here's an example of what the manifest looks like with this change (some of the lines have been truncated for brevity):

```
            CACHE MANIFEST
./index.html
./jqtouch/jqtouch.css
./jqtouch/jqtouch.js
...
./themes/jqt/img/toolbar.png
./themes/jqt/img/whiteButton.png
./themes/jqt/theme.css
# Hash: ddaf5ebda18991c4a9da16c10f4e474a
```

The net result of all of this business is that changing a single character inside of any file in the entire directory tree will insert a new hash string into the manifest. This means that any edits we do to any Kilo files will essentially modify the manifest file, which in turn will trigger a download the next time a user launches the app. Pretty nifty, eh?

Debugging

It can be tough to debug apps that use the offline application cache because there's very little visibility into what is going on. You find yourself constantly wondering if your files have downloaded, or if you are viewing remote or local resources. Plus, switching your device between online and offline modes is not the snappiest procedure and can really slow down the develop, test, debug cycle.

There are two things you can do to help determine what's going on when things aren't playing nice: set up some console logging in JavaScript, and browse the application cache database.

> If you want to see what's happening from the web server's perspective, you can monitor its logfiles. For example, if you are running a web server on a Mac computer, you can open a Terminal window (Applications→Utilities→Terminal) and run these commands (the $ is the Terminal shell prompt and should not be typed):
>
> ```
> $ cd /var/log/apache2/
> $ tail -f access_log
> ```
>
> This will display the web server's log entries, showing information such as the date and time a document was accessed, as well as the name of the document. When you are done, press Control-C to stop following the log.

The JavaScript Console

Adding the following JavaScript to your web apps during development will make your life a lot easier, and can actually help you internalize the process of what is going on. The following script will send feedback to the console and free you from having to constantly refresh the browser window (you can store the script in a *.js* file that your HTML document references via the script element's src attribute):

```javascript
// Convenience array of status values❶
var cacheStatusValues = [];
cacheStatusValues[0] = 'uncached';
cacheStatusValues[1] = 'idle';
cacheStatusValues[2] = 'checking';
cacheStatusValues[3] = 'downloading';
cacheStatusValues[4] = 'updateready';
cacheStatusValues[5] = 'obsolete';

// Listeners for all possible events❷
var cache = window.applicationCache;
cache.addEventListener('cached', logEvent, false);
cache.addEventListener('checking', logEvent, false);
cache.addEventListener('downloading', logEvent, false);
cache.addEventListener('error', logEvent, false);
cache.addEventListener('noupdate', logEvent, false);
cache.addEventListener('obsolete', logEvent, false);
cache.addEventListener('progress', logEvent, false);
cache.addEventListener('updateready', logEvent, false);

// Log every event to the console
function logEvent(e) {❸
    var online, status, type, message;
    online = (navigator.onLine) ? 'yes' : 'no';
    status = cacheStatusValues[cache.status];
    type = e.type;
```

```
        message = 'online: ' + online;
        message+= ', event: ' + type;
        message+= ', status: ' + status;
        if (type == 'error' && navigator.onLine) {
            message+= ' (prolly a syntax error in manifest)';
        }
        console.log(message);❹
    }

    // Swap in newly downloaded files when update is ready
    window.applicationCache.addEventListener(
        'updateready',
        function(){
            window.applicationCache.swapCache();
            console.log('swap cache has been called');
        },
        false
    );

    // Check for manifest changes every 10 seconds
    setInterval(function(){cache.update()}, 10000);
```

This might look like a lot of code, but there really isn't that much going on here:

❶ The first seven lines are just me setting up an array of status values for the application cache object. There are six possible values defined by the HTML5 spec, and here I'm mapping their integer values to a short description (e.g., status 3 means "downloading"). I've included them to make the logging more descriptive down in the logEvent function.

❷ In the next chunk of code, I'm setting up an event listener for every possible event defined by the spec. Each one calls the logEvent function.

❸ The logEvent function takes the event as input and makes a few simple calculations in order to compose a descriptive log message. Note that if the event type is **error** and the user is online, there is probably a syntax error in the remote manifest. Syntax errors are extremely easy to make in the manifest because all of the paths have to be valid. If you rename or move a file but forget to update the manifest, future updates will fail.

❹ Once I have my message composed, I send it to the console.

You can view the console messages in desktop Safari by selecting Develop→Show Error Console. You can view the console messages in the iPhone Simulator by going to Settings→Safari→Developer and turning the Debug Console on. When debugging is turned on, Mobile Safari displays a header above the location bar (Figure 6-7) that allows you to navigate to the debugging console (Figure 6-8).

Figure 6-7. Mobile Safari with debugging turned on

Figure 6-8. Mobile Safari debugging console

If you don't see the Develop menu in the Safari menu bar, open your Safari application preferences, click the Advanced tab, and make sure that "Show Develop menu in menu bar" is checked.

If you load the web page in your browser and then open the console, you'll see new messages appear every 10 seconds (Figure 6-9). If you don't see anything, update the version number in *demo.manifest* and reload the page in your browser *twice*. I strongly encourage you to play around with this until you really have a feel for what's going on. You can tinker around with the manifest (change the contents and save it, rename it, move it to another directory, etc.) and watch the results of your actions pop into the console like magic.

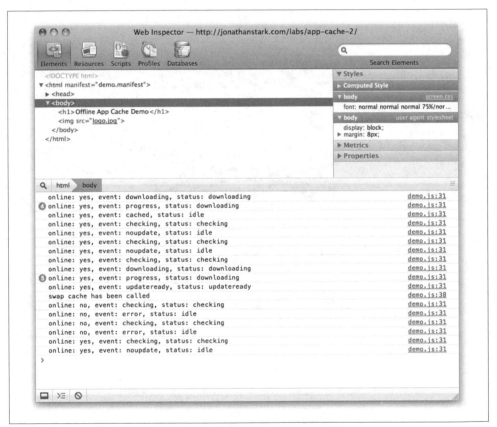

Figure 6-9. The console.log() function can be used to send debugging messages to the JavaScript console

The Application Cache Database

If you are having serious trouble debugging your offline web app, there is a way to get under the hood and see what's going on. If you load your app in the iPhone Simulator, it stores the cached resources in a SQLite database that you can peruse with the sqlite3 command-line interface. Of course, having some knowledge of SQL would help here, but you can get pretty far by mimicking the examples in this section.

 You will need to install the iPhone SDK from Apple in order to get the simulator. You can get the SDK by registering as an Apple developer at *http://developer.apple.com/iphone/*. Registration costs nothing, but you will need to enroll in an iPhone developer program (note that an Apple developer is different from an iPhone developer) if you want to submit your apps to the App Store.

On my machine, the iPhone Simulator app cache database is located here:

```
/Users/jstark/Library/Application Support/iPhone
Simulator/User/Library/Caches/com.apple.WebAppCache/ApplicationCache.db
```

 The *com.apple.WebAppCache* directory and *ApplicationCache.db* database will not exist unless you have loaded the web application on the iPhone Simulator at least once.

Using the sqlite3 command-line interface, you can poke around in the database to get an idea of what's going on. First, you have to connect to the database. Open the Terminal (Applications→Utilities→Terminal) and type the commands that follow. (The $ is the Terminal prompt and should not be typed.)

```
$ cd "$HOME/Library/Application Support/iPhone Simulator"
$ cd User/Library/Caches/com.apple.WebAppCache/
$ sqlite3 ApplicationCache.db
```

 On the Mac, desktop Safari's application cache can be found in a directory adjacent to your temporary directory. You can get to it in the terminal with:

```
$ cd $TMPDIR/../-Caches-/com.apple.Safari/
$ sqlite3 ApplicationCache.db
```

Once connected, you'll see something like:

```
SQLite version 3.6.17
Enter ".help" for instructions
Enter SQL statements terminated with a ";"
sqlite>
```

Now you can type SQLite control statements and arbitrary SQL commands at the `sqlite>` prompt. To see a list of SQLite control statements, type `.help` at the prompt. You'll see a long list of commands, of which these are the most important for our purposes:

```
.exit                 Exit this program
.header(s) ON|OFF     Turn display of headers on or off
.help                 Show this message
.mode MODE ?TABLE?    Set output mode where MODE is one of:
                        csv      Comma-separated values
                        column   Left-aligned columns.  (See .width)
                        html     HTML <table> code
                        insert   SQL insert statements for TABLE
                        line     One value per line
                        list     Values delimited by .separator string
                        tabs     Tab-separated values
                        tcl      TCL list elements
.quit                 Exit this program
.tables ?PATTERN?     List names of tables matching a LIKE pattern
```

To retrieve a list of tables used in the cache manifest database, use the `.tables` command:

```
sqlite> .tables
CacheEntries          CacheResourceData     CacheWhitelistURLs  FallbackURLs
CacheGroups           CacheResources        Caches
```

Before I start querying the tables, I'm going to set `.headers` to `ON`, which will add field names to the output, and set `.mode` to `line` to make things easier to read. Type the commands shown in bold (`sqlite>` is the SQLite prompt):

```
sqlite> .headers on
sqlite> .mode line
```

CacheGroups is the top level of the data model. It contains a row for each version of the manifest. Type the command shown in bold (don't forget the `;`):

```
sqlite> select * from CacheGroups;
              id = 1
manifestHostHash = 2669513278
     manifestURL = http://jonathanstark.com/labs/kilo10/kilo.manifest
     newestCache = 7

              id = 2
manifestHostHash = 2669513278
     manifestURL = http://jonathanstark.com/labs/cache-manifest-bug/test.manifest
     newestCache = 6

              id = 5
manifestHostHash = 2669513278
     manifestURL = http://jonathanstark.com/labs/kilo11/kilo.manifest
     newestCache = 13

              id = 6
manifestHostHash = 2669513278
```

```
manifestURL = http://jonathanstark.com/labs/app-cache-3/demo.manifest
newestCache = 14
```

As you can see, I have four cache groups on my machine. You probably only have one
at this point. The fields break down like this:

id

A unique autoincrement serial number assigned to the row. Every time Mobile
Safari inserts a row into this table, this number is incremented. If, for some reason,
Mobile Safari needs to delete a row, you will see gaps in the sequence.

manifestHostHash

Used with manifestURL to uniquely identify the cache.

manifestURL

The location of the remote manifest file.

newestCache

This is a Caches row ID (i.e., a *foreign key* to the Caches table) that indicates which
cache to use.

A column in a database table is considered a *key* when it identifies
something. For example, a *unique key* identifies a row in the table un-
ambiguously. A *primary key* is a unique key that has been designated as
the key you use to identify a row. For example, two columns are poten-
tial unique keys because there is only one row in the CacheGroups table
for any given value of these columns: id and manifestURL. However,
id is a simple numeric key, and it's very fast to make comparisons to it
(and it requires less storage for other tables to refer to it). So, id is both
a unique key and the primary key for the CacheGroups table.

A foreign key is a link from one table to another. The cacheGroup column
in the Caches table (discussed next) identifies a row in the CacheGroups
table, establishing a link from a row in one table to the other.

Now, switch to column mode and select all rows from the Caches table:

```
sqlite> .mode column
sqlite> select * from Caches;
id          cacheGroup
----------  ----------
6           2
7           1
13          5
14          6
```

The Caches table has just two fields: id (primary key for the Caches row), and
cacheGroup (foreign key that links a Caches id to a row in the CacheGroups table). If
Safari were in the process of downloading a new cache, there would be two Cache rows
for the CacheGroup (one current, one temporary). In all other cases, there is only one
Cache row per CacheGroup.

Next, let's select all of the rows from the `CacheEntries` table:

```
sqlite> select * from CacheEntries;
cache       type        resource
----------  ----------  ----------
6           1           67
6           4           68
6           2           69
7           4           70
7           4           71
7           4           72
7           4           73
7           2           74
7           4           75
7           4           76
7           4           77
7           1           78
7           4           79
13          4           160
13          4           161
13          4           162
13          4           163
13          2           164
13          4           165
13          4           166
13          4           167
13          4           168
13          1           169
13          4           170
13          4           171
13          4           172
13          4           173
13          4           174
13          4           175
14          4           176
14          16          177
14          4           178
14          1           179
14          4           180
14          2           181
```

Not much to look at here. Just two foreign keys (`cache`, which is a foreign key to the `Caches.id` column, and `resource`, which is a foreign key to `CacheResources.id`) and a `type` field. I'll redo that query with a `join` to the `CacheResources` table so you can see how the type corresponds to the actual files. Notice that first I set the column widths so the URLs don't get cut off (the `...>` prompt indicates that I pressed Return before finishing the statement with the `;` terminator):

```
sqlite> .width 5 4 8 24 80
sqlite> select cache, type, resource, mimetype, url
   ...> from CacheEntries,CacheResources where resource=id order by type;
--  -- ---  ----------  --------------------------------------------------------
6   1  67   text/htm... http://jonathanstark.com/labs/cache-manifest-bug/
7   1  78   text/htm... http://jonathanstark.com/labs/kilo10/#home
13  1  169  text/htm... http://jonathanstark.com/labs/kilo11/#home
```

```
14   1  179 text/htm... http://jonathanstark.com/labs/app-cache-3/
6    2  69  text/cac... http://jonathanstark.com/labs/cache-manifest-bug/test.manifest
7    2  74  text/cac... http://jonathanstark.com/labs/kilo10/kilo.manifest
13   2  164 text/cac... http://jonathanstark.com/labs/kilo11/kilo.manifest
14   2  181 text/cac... http://jonathanstark.com/labs/app-cache-3/demo.manifest
6    4  68  image/pn... http://jonathanstark.com/labs/kilo10/icon.png
7    4  70  text/css... http://jonathanstark.com/labs/kilo10/jqtouch/jqtouch.css
7    4  71  image/pn... http://jonathanstark.com/labs/kilo10/icon.png
7    4  72  text/css... http://jonathanstark.com/labs/kilo10/themes/jqt/theme.css
7    4  73  image/pn... http://jonathanstark.com/labs/kilo10/startupScreen.png
7    4  75  applicat... http://jonathanstark.com/labs/kilo10/jqtouch/jqtouch.js
7    4  76  applicat... http://jonathanstark.com/labs/kilo10/kilo.js
7    4  77  applicat... http://jonathanstark.com/labs/kilo10/jqtouch/jquery.js
7    4  79  image/x-... http://jonathanstark.com/favicon.ico
13   4  160 applicat... http://jonathanstark.com/labs/kilo11/kilo.js
13   4  161 text/css... http://jonathanstark.com/labs/kilo11/jqtouch/jqtouch.css
13   4  162 image/pn... http://jonathanstark.com/labs/kilo11/icon.png
13   4  163 image/x-... http://jonathanstark.com/favicon.ico
13   4  165 image/pn... http://jonathanstark.com/labs/kilo11/themes/jqt/img/button.png
13   4  166 image/pn... http://jonathanstark.com/labs/kilo11/themes/jqt/
img/chevron.png
13   4  167 text/css... http://jonathanstark.com/labs/kilo11/themes/jqt/theme.css
13   4  168 applicat... http://jonathanstark.com/labs/kilo11/jqtouch/jquery.js
13   4  170 applicat... http://jonathanstark.com/labs/kilo11/jqtouch/jqtouch.js
13   4  171 image/pn... http://jonathanstark.com/labs/kilo11/themes/jqt/
img/back_button.png
13   4  172 image/pn... http://jonathanstark.com/labs/kilo11/themes/jqt/img/toolbar.png
13   4  173 image/pn... http://jonathanstark.com/labs/kilo11/startupScreen.png
13   4  174 image/pn... http://jonathanstark.com/labs/kilo11/themes/jqt/
img/back_button_clicked.png
13   4  175 image/pn... http://jonathanstark.com/labs/kilo11/themes/jqt/
img/button_clicked.png
14   4  176 text/htm... http://jonathanstark.com/labs/app-cache-3/index.html
14   4  178 applicat... http://jonathanstark.com/labs/app-cache-3/scripts/demo.js
14   4  180 text/css... http://jonathanstark.com/labs/app-cache-3/styles/screen.css
14  16  177 image/jp... http://jonathanstark.com/labs/app-cache-3/images/offline.jpg
```

Reviewing this list reveals that type 1 indicates a host file, type 2 is a manifest file, type 4 is any normal static resource, and type 16 is a fallback resource.

Let's switch back to line mode and pull some data from the CacheResources table to see what is going on in there. Here's resource row 73 (if you're trying this out yourself, replace 73 with a valid id value from the results you got in the previous query of the CacheResources table):

```
sqlite> .mode line
sqlite> select * from CacheResources where id=73;
              id = 73
             url = http://jonathanstark.com/labs/kilo10/startupScreen.png
      statusCode = 200
     responseURL = http://jonathanstark.com/labs/kilo10/startupScreen.png
        mimeType = image/png
textEncodingName =
         headers = Date:Thu, 24 Sep 2009 19:16:09 GMT
X-Pad:avoid browser bug
```

```
Connection:close
Content-Length:12303
Last-Modified:Fri, 18 Sep 2009 05:02:26 GMT
Server:Apache/2.2.8 (Fedora)
Etag:"52c88b-300f-473d309c45c80"
Content-Type:image/png
Accept-Ranges:bytes

            data = 73
```

If you are familiar with the way HTTP requests work, you'll recognize that this is exactly the data that you'd need to fake a network response. Here Mobile Safari has all the info needed to serve up a PNG file to the browser (or in this case, to itself; it is storing the information needed to reproduce the behavior of the web server that originally provided the file).

Well, in fact it has all of the info except for the actual image data. The image data is stored in a blob field in `CacheResourceData`. I'd include it here, but it's binary and not much to look at. It's interesting to note that even text datafiles (HTML, CSS, JavaScript, etc.) and the like are stored as binary data in the blob field in `CacheResourceData`.

Let's take a look at the `CacheWhitelistURLs` table, which contains all the elements identified in the `NETWORK:` section of the manifest:

```
sqlite> .width 80 5
sqlite> .mode column
sqlite> select * from CacheWhitelistURLs;
url                                                                              cache
-------------------------------------------------------------------------------- ------
http://jonathanstark.com/labs/kilo10/themes/jqt/img/back_button.png             7
http://jonathanstark.com/labs/kilo10/themes/jqt/img/back_button_clicked.png     7
http://jonathanstark.com/labs/kilo10/themes/jqt/img/button.png                  7
http://jonathanstark.com/labs/kilo10/themes/jqt/img/button_clicked.png          7
http://jonathanstark.com/labs/kilo10/themes/jqt/img/chevron.png                 7
http://jonathanstark.com/labs/kilo10/themes/jqt/img/toolbar.png                 7
```

Here we just have the cache `id` and the URL to the online resource. If cache `id` 7 is requested by the browser, these six images will be retrieved from their remote location if the user is online. If the user is offline, they will show up as broken links because they are not stored locally. It's worth noting that the URLs have been fully expanded to absolute URLs, even though they were listed in the manifest as relative URLs.

And finally, let's take a look at the `FallbackURLs` table (everything from the `FALLBACK:` section of the manifest):

```
sqlite> .mode line
sqlite> select * from FallbackURLs;
  namespace = http://jonathanstark.com/labs/app-cache-3/images/
fallbackURL = http://jonathanstark.com/labs/app-cache-3/images/offline.jpg
      cache = 14
```

As you can see, I currently have only one row in the `FallbackURLs` table. If cache `id` 14 is requested by the browser, and any URLs that begin with `http://jonathanstark.com/labs/app-cache-3/images/` fail for whatever reason (the user is offline, images are missing, etc.), the `fallbackURL` will be used instead.

I apologize if this section is a bit complex, but at this point it's all we've got. Maybe browser vendors will implement some sort of user interface that will allow us to browse the application cache—similar to those for the local storage and client-side database—but until that time comes, this is our only option for prowling around in the depths of client-side storage.

What You've Learned

In this chapter, you've learned how to give users access to a web app, even when they have no connection to the Internet. This offline mode applies whether the app is loaded in Mobile Safari, or launched in full screen mode from a Web Clip icon on the desktop. With this new addition to your programming toolbox, you now have the ability to create a full-screen, offline app that is virtually indistinguishable from a native application downloaded from the App Store.

Of course, a pure web app such as this is still limited by the security constraints that exist for all web apps. For example, a web app can't access the Address Book, the camera, the accelerometer, or vibration on the iPhone. In the next chapter, I'll address these issues and more with the assistance of an open source project called PhoneGap.

Going Native

Our web app can now do many of the things that a native app can do: launch from the home screen, run in full screen mode, store data locally on the iPhone, and operate in offline mode. We've formatted it nicely for the device and set up native-looking animations to provide feedback and context to the user.

However, there are still two things that our app cannot do: it can't access the device features and hardware (e.g., geolocation, accelerometer, sound, and vibration), and it can't be submitted to the iTunes App Store. In this chapter, you will learn how to use PhoneGap to bridge this, um...gap on your, ah...phone. Clever name, that!

Intro to PhoneGap

PhoneGap is an open source development tool created by Nitobi (*http://www.nitobi .com/*) to act as a bridge between web applications and mobile devices. iPhone, Google Android, and BlackBerry operating systems are currently supported, and Nokia and Windows Mobile are in development.

In spite of its high profile, the iPhone is not even close to being the most widely used mobile device. The mobile landscape is littered with devices, platforms, and operating systems. If you are a web developer, you might be familiar with the pain of testing 10 or so browser versions across 10 or so operating system versions. Multiply that by 100, and you have mobile. There is simply no cost-effective way to develop and test across all of the possible combinations.

Thanks to Apple, it's now clear that there is a market for devices that offer a full-featured web browsing experience. As more vendors include high-quality browsers on their phones, the work that we've done here becomes more valuable. By building a web app, we have effectively skirted much of the complexity of mobile development. We can have one codebase deployed to multiple devices and platforms.

Of course, different devices have different features. Maybe a particular phone doesn't support multitouch, or doesn't have an accelerometer. Even when devices do have the same features, each has its own way of exposing these features to the developer.

PhoneGap abstracts the APIs for the most widely available mobile phone features so mobile application developers can use the same code everywhere. You still need to deploy your app manually using the SDK provided by the vendor, but you don't need to change your application code.

> There are other projects and products available that serve the same basic purpose as PhoneGap, such as RhoMobile (*http://rhomobile.com/*) and Titanium Mobile (*http://www.appcelerator.com/*). I'm not familiar enough with them to compare and contrast, but you might want to check them out in case one suits your needs better than PhoneGap.

Since this is an iPhone book, I'm going to focus on the iPhone portion of PhoneGap. Just be aware that you can also potentially deploy your app to Android, BlackBerry, and Windows Mobile devices with little or no modification.

> In the case of the iPhone, this SDK requirement means that you are going to need a Mac with Xcode installed, and you are going to have to pay money to join the iPhone Developer Program. Sorry about that. You can get the SDK by registering as an Apple developer at *http://developer.ap ple.com/iphone/*. Registration costs nothing, but you will need to enroll in an iPhone developer program if you want to submit your apps to the App Store or even run them on your own phone. You can, however, use the free SDK to test your apps in the iPhone Simulator, which is included with the iPhone SDK. After you've registered as an iPhone developer, return to *http://developer.apple.com/iphone/*, log in, and download the iPhone SDK. The iPhone SDK includes Xcode, which is the development environment that you'll use to test your apps in the simulator, run them on your own iPhone, and submit them to the App Store.

To get started with PhoneGap, you first need to download it. You can do so by visiting *http://github.com/phonegap/phonegap* and clicking the download button (Figure 7-1). Assuming you're on a Mac, you'll probably want to download the ZIP version. When the download completes, unarchive it to your desktop (Figure 7-2).

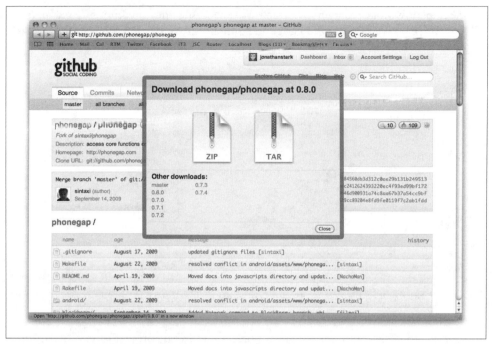

Figure 7-1. Download the latest version of PhoneGap from GitHub

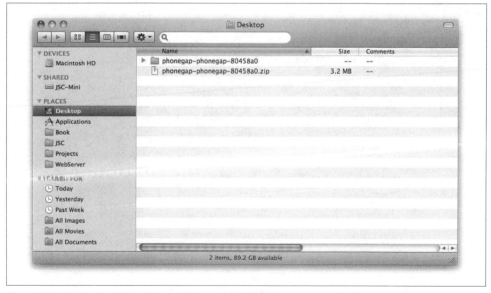

Figure 7-2. Unzip the PhoneGap archive to your desktop

PhoneGap download contains a bunch of device-specific directories (e.g., *android*, *iphone*, *blackberry*, *windows mobile*), and some library and utility files and directories (Figure 7-3). The only one we'll be looking at is the *iphone* directory.

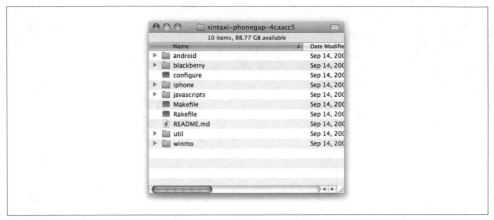

Figure 7-3. The top-level PhoneGap directory contains subdirectories for various mobile platforms

The *iphone* directory contains the starter files for an Xcode project (Figure 7-4). There is nothing magical about these files, other than the fact that they were written *for* you rather than *by* you; they're just the kind of garden-variety source files that you'd find in any Xcode project.

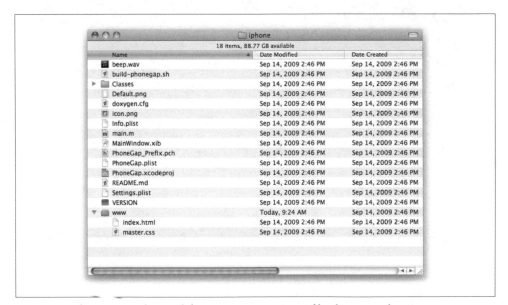

Figure 7-4. PhoneGap's iPhone subdirectory contains starter files for an Xcode project

Inside the *iphone* directory, there is a directory named *www*. You can think of this as the web root of the application. By default, it contains two sample files named *index.html* and *master.css*. These are used as the demo PhoneGap application. We don't need them, so you can delete them both (Figure 7-5).

Name	Date Modified	Date Created
beep.wav	Sep 14, 2009 2:46 PM	Sep 14, 2009 2:46 PM
build-phonegap.sh	Sep 14, 2009 2:46 PM	Sep 14, 2009 2:46 PM
▶ Classes	Sep 14, 2009 2:46 PM	Sep 14, 2009 2:46 PM
Default.png	Sep 14, 2009 2:46 PM	Sep 14, 2009 2:46 PM
doxygen.cfg	Sep 14, 2009 2:46 PM	Sep 14, 2009 2:46 PM
icon.png	Sep 14, 2009 2:46 PM	Sep 14, 2009 2:46 PM
Info.plist	Sep 14, 2009 2:46 PM	Sep 14, 2009 2:46 PM
main.m	Sep 14, 2009 2:46 PM	Sep 14, 2009 2:46 PM
MainWindow.xib	Sep 14, 2009 2:46 PM	Sep 14, 2009 2:46 PM
PhoneGap_Prefix.pch	Sep 14, 2009 2:46 PM	Sep 14, 2009 2:46 PM
PhoneGap.plist	Sep 14, 2009 2:46 PM	Sep 14, 2009 2:46 PM
PhoneGap.xcodeproj	Sep 14, 2009 2:46 PM	Sep 14, 2009 2:46 PM
README.md	Sep 14, 2009 2:46 PM	Sep 14, 2009 2:46 PM
Settings.plist	Sep 14, 2009 2:46 PM	Sep 14, 2009 2:46 PM
VERSION	Sep 14, 2009 2:46 PM	Sep 14, 2009 2:46 PM
▼ www	Today, 9:24 AM	Sep 14, 2009 2:46 PM
index.html	Sep 14, 2009 2:46 PM	Sep 14, 2009 2:46 PM
master.css	Sep 14, 2009 2:46 PM	Sep 14, 2009 2:46 PM

iphone — 2 of 18 selected, 88.77 GB available

Figure 7-5. Delete the two default files from the www directory

Next, copy all of the files from the Kilo app that we've been working on into the *www* directory (on the Mac, hold down Option while dragging files to make a copy). Don't change your folder structure or naming; just drop everything in there as is (Figure 7-6).

 If you have added a manifest link to the html tag in *index.html* as described in Chapter 6, you must remove it. It's unnecessary when using PhoneGap and may cause performance problems.

Next, go into your *index.html* file, add the following line to the <head> section, and save the file:

```
<script type="text/javascript" src="phonegap.js" charset="utf-8"></script>
```

You don't need to copy the *phonegap.js* file into your *www* directory. When you build your app, Xcode takes care of this for you.

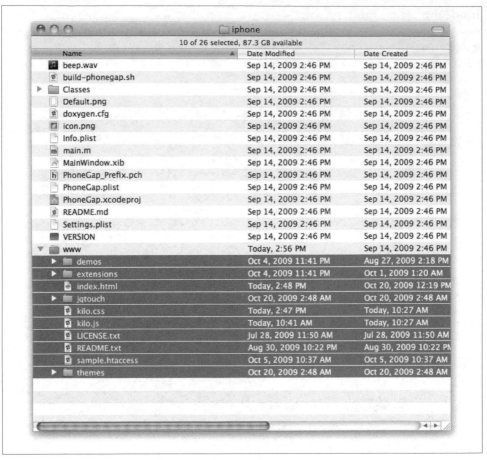

Figure 7-6. Copy your entire web app into the www directory

 Make sure the main page for your app is named *index.html*; otherwise, PhoneGap won't know what file to launch.

Unbelievably, we're almost ready to test our app. Open the project in Xcode by double-clicking the *PhoneGap.xcodeproj* file in the Finder. Once the project window is open, make sure you have the most recent version of the iPhone Simulator (3.1.2 as of this writing) selected as your active SDK and then click the Build and Run button (Figure 7-7). After about 10 seconds, the iPhone Simulator should appear and launch your app.

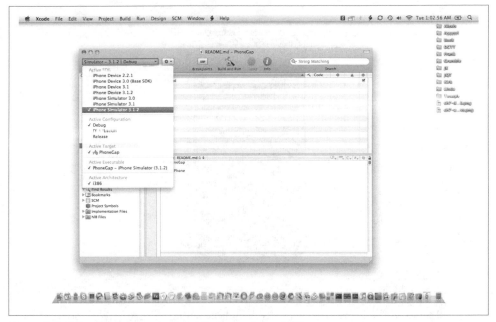

Figure 7-7. Select iPhone Simulator 3.1.2 as your active SDK

> If the simulator does not launch, it means there is an error in your project. Look for a red number in the bottom right corner of the Xcode window; this is the number of errors encountered. Click the number for details about the error, and then review these steps to figure out where things went wrong. If you run into a problem you can't resolve, visit the PhoneGap community resources at *http://phonegap.com/community*. Search through the wiki and Google Group for answers to your problem before posting a question. If you do post a question, include as much information as possible about the error.

Your app should now be running in the iPhone Simulator as a native app. This may seem like no big deal, because the app will look and feel just like the full-screen web app that we had running in Chapter 6. However, there is a profound difference: namely, that we can now start accessing device features that were previously unavailable. Before we get to that, though, we need to do a bit of cleanup.

Using the Screen's Full Height

You'll notice that there is a 40px gap at the bottom of the window (Figure 7-8). This occurs because jQTouch does not realize that we are running in full screen mode, so it's allowing room for the Safari toolbar. This makes sense from jQTouch's perspective, because the app technically isn't running as a full-screen web app. But it is running as

Figure 7-8. You'll notice a 40px gap at the bottom of the screen

a native app, and therefore has access to the whole screen. Fortunately, the fix is easy. Just open *kilo.js* and add the following code to the document ready function:

```
if (typeof(PhoneGap) != 'undefined') {
    $('body > *').css({minHeight: '460px !important'});
}
```

> Now that you've opened your PhoneGap project in Xcode, you might want to give Xcode's built-in editor a try. To edit the *kilo.js* file in Xcode, make sure the PhoneGap group is open in the Groups & Files panel on the left side of the Xcode window. Expand the *www* folder and click *kilo.js* to open it in Xcode's editor.

This code uses the `typeof` operator to make sure the `PhoneGap` object has been defined. If the code is running inside of PhoneGap, this conditional will evaluate to `true`. If the code is launched as a web app, the `PhoneGap` object will be undefined and the conditional will evaluate to `false`.

When the app is launched with PhoneGap, the immediate children of the HTML body element will be given a minimum height of 460px. To make sure that the declaration takes effect, I've added the `!important` directive to override any conflicting instructions elsewhere in the stylesheets. Now the app will completely fill the window when launched (Figure 7-9).

Figure 7-9. After the body height is changed from 420px to 460px, the app takes up the whole screen

Customizing the Title and Icon

Next, we need to change the default name and icon for the app. By default, PhoneGap apps are called "PhoneGap" and have a blue icon with a ladder on it (Figure 7-10).

Figure 7-10. The default name and icon for our app

To change the app name on the home screen, open the project in Xcode by double-clicking the *PhoneGap.xcodeproj* file in the Finder. Once it's open, go to PhoneGap→Config→Info.plist in the Groups & Files panel. The *Info.plist* file should be displayed in the bottom-right panel of the window.

You should see that the bundle display name is set to PhoneGap (Figure 7-11). Double-click PhoneGap and change it to Kilo (Figure 7-12). Then save the file, clean the project (by clicking Build→Clean), and click the Build and Run button. The iPhone Simulator should open and launch the app. Click the home button in the simulator to return to the home screen and note that the app name has been updated from PhoneGap to Kilo (Figure 7-13).

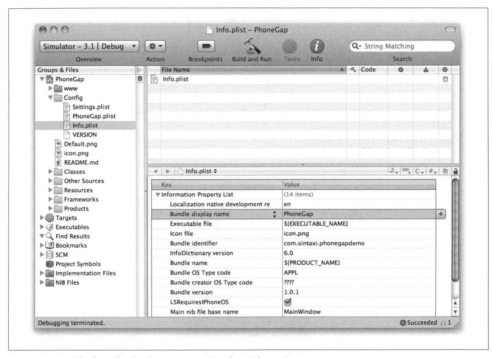

Figure 7-11. The bundle display name in Xcode is PhoneGap

Next, we need to change the home screen icon from the PhoneGap default (the ladder, pictured in Figure 7-10) to our custom icon. The file format for both the app icon and the Web Clip icon is a 57px × 57px PNG, so you can use the exact same web app icon that you created for the home screen icon in "Adding an Icon to the Home Screen" on page 46.

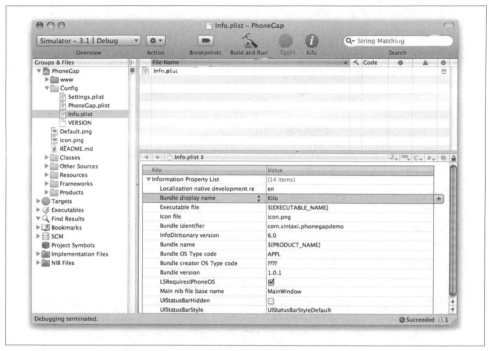

Figure 7-12. The bundle display name is now set to the name of our app (Kilo)

Figure 7-13. The new bundle display name now appears on the iPhone home screen

The only difference is that with the Web Clip icon, we can prevent the iPhone from adding gloss to the graphic by toggling the `addGlossToIcon` setting in jQTouch; this setting will have no effect in PhoneGap. To prevent adding gloss to your icon in PhoneGap, select *Config/Info.plist* in the Groups & Files panel of the main Xcode window and check the box next to `UIPrerenderedIcon` in *Info.plist* (you may need to add this to *Info.plist*; see "Adding Settings to Info.plist" next for instructions).

Adding Settings to Info.plist

If you don't see the `UIPrerenderedIcon` option in *Info.plist*, you can add it by following these steps:

1. Select Config/Info.plist in the Groups & Files panel of the main Xcode window (Figure 7-14).
2. Control-click or right-click the last item in *Info.plist* to display the contextual menu.
3. Select Add Row from the contextual menu (Figure 7-15).
4. Type `UIPrerenderedIcon` in the key field (Figure 7-16).
5. Press the Enter key to save your entry. The row should become highlighted (Figure 7-17).
6. Control-click or right-click the highlighted row to display the contextual menu again, and select Boolean from the Value Type submenu (Figure 7-18). A checkbox should appear in the value column.
7. Check the checkbox to tell Xcode not to add gloss to your icon (Figure 7-19).

Clean your project (by clicking Build→Clean), and when you build and run it, your icon will appear without the gloss effect added.

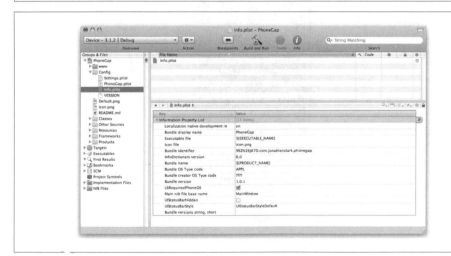

Figure 7-14. Select Config/Info.plist in the Groups & Files panel of the main Xcode window

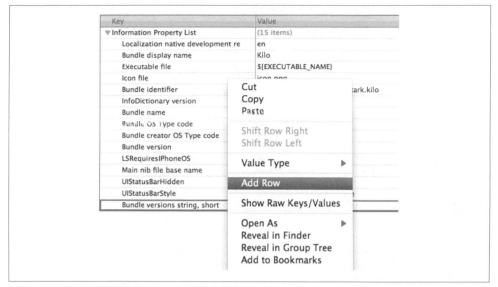

Figure 7-15. Select Add Row from the contextual menu

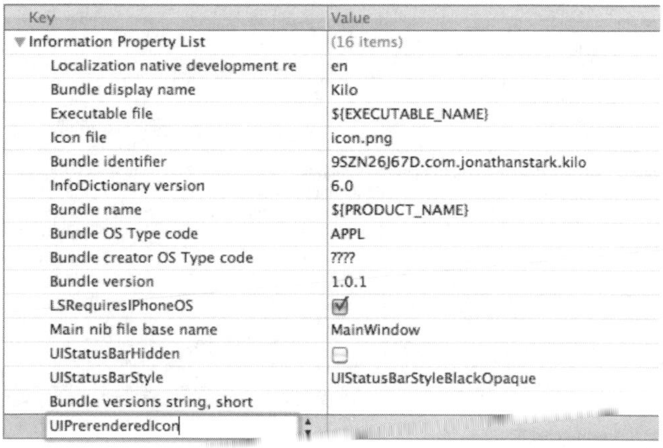

Figure 7-16. Type UIPrerenderedIcon in the key field

The default PhoneGap home screen icon is named *icon.png* and is located in PhoneGap's *iphone* directory (Figure 7-20). Replace the default icon file with your custom file (Figures 7-21 and 7-22), clean the project (click Build→Clean), and click the Build and Run button. The iPhone Simulator should open and launch the app. Click the home button in the simulator to return to the home screen, and note that the app icon has been updated to a chocolate frosted donut with jimmies on a pink background (Figure 7-23).

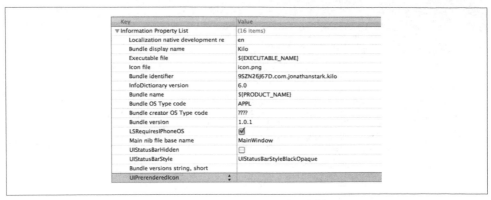

Figure 7-17. Press the Enter key to save your entry in the key field

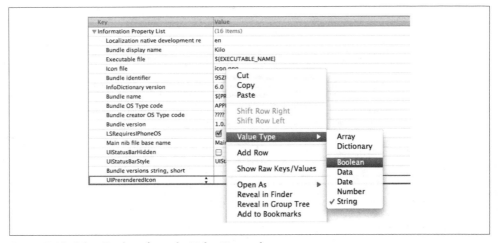

Figure 7-18. Select Boolean from the Value Type submenu

Figure 7-19. Check the checkbox to tell Xcode not to add gloss to your icon

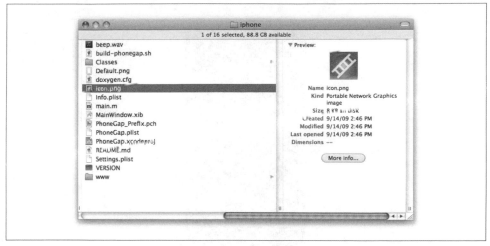

Figure 7-20. The default home screen icon is a white ladder on a blue background

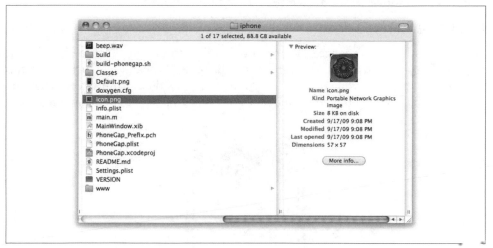

Figure 7-21. The custom home screen icon is a chocolate frosted donut with jimmies on a pink background

Figure 7-22. Replace icon.png in iphone directory with your own custom 57px × 57px png graphic

Figure 7-23. Our custom app icon now appears on the iPhone home screen

Creating a Startup Screen

Next we need to change the startup screen from the PhoneGap default
(Figure 7-24) to our custom startup screen. Back in "Providing a Custom Startup
Graphic" on page 49, you created a PNG file to serve as the startup screen when the
web app is launched in full screen mode from a Web Clip icon on the home screen.

Figure 7-24. We need to change the default startup graphic for the app

For full-screen web apps that use a gray or black status bar, this graphic needs to be 320px × 460px, and for apps that use a black-translucent status bar, it must be 320px × 480px (20 pixels taller).

With PhoneGap, the startup screen has to be 320px × 480px regardless of what type of status bar is used. So if you created a 320px × 460px full-screen graphic, add 20px to the height.

The default PhoneGap startup graphic is named *Default.png* and is located in PhoneGap's *iphone* directory (Figure 7-25). Replace the default startup graphic with your custom graphic (as shown in Figures 7-26 and 7-27) as shown in Figure 7-27, clean the project, and click the Build and Run button. The iPhone Simulator should open and launch the app, and you should see the custom graphic displayed (Figure 7-28).

Figure 7-25. The default launch graphic says PhoneGap in gray text on a white background

Installing Your App on the iPhone

In the next section, we'll add sound, vibration, alerts, and more to the Kilo example application. Some of these features can't be tested in the iPhone Simulator, so you need to get Kilo installed on an actual iPhone before you can test any of this.

Figure 7-26. The custom launch graphic says Kilo in gray text on a black background

Figure 7-27. Replace Default.png in the iphone directory with the custom 320px × 480px PNG graphic

Figure 7-28. Our custom startup graphic now appears when the app is launched

To install an app on the iPhone, Apple requires that the app, the phone, and the developer (you) all be uniquely identified. These three pieces of data are combined in a file called a "provisioning profile" that you will add to Xcode.

In order to generate a provisioning profile, you must first be a member of the iPhone Developer Program. You then run the Development Provisioning Assistant (DPA) found in the iPhone Developer Program Portal section of the iPhone developer site (*http://developer.apple.com/iphone/*). You'll be making a couple of trips into the Keychain Access application (located in */Applications/Utilities*) to create *certificate signing requests* and to install signed certificates that you download from the portal into your own keychain. The DPA does an excellent job walking you through the steps needed to create and install your provisioning profile, so I won't rehash the instructions here. However, I will give you some pointers:

- When I first started with iPhone app development, I made a few test App IDs in the Program Portal, assuming that I could later edit or delete them once I figured out how things worked. Well, I was wrong; you can't edit or delete App IDs. This means that two years later, I'm still staring at "JSC Temp App ID" when I log in to the developer portal. If you are anything like me, this will drive you crazy, so don't make the same mistake!

- Keep your input brief but descriptive in the DPA. If your descriptors are too vague, you'll get confused as you add more items. If descriptors are too long, they'll be truncated in the online interface. Try to keep things to a max of about 20 characters.

- When prompted for an App ID description, just use the name of your app (and possibly a version number, if you are planning on having multiple versions active in the App Store at the same time—e.g., Kilo2).

- When prompted for a device description, include the type of device (iPhone, iPod touch, etc.) and the hardware version (1G, 2G, 3G, 3GS, etc.). Don't include the OS version, because this can change without invalidating the provisioning profile. Bear in mind that if you end up making beta versions of the app available to testers, you'll also want to include an owner identifier (for example, you could use initials: ELS iPhone 3GS, JSC iPhone 2G, JSC iPhone 3G, JSC Touch 1G, etc.).

- When prompted for a profile description, combine the name of the app with the target device (e.g., Kilo2 on JSC iPhone 3GS).

Once you've created your provisioning profile, you must download it and drag it onto Xcode's dock icon to make it available to your device. This brings up the organizer window. If you have multiple apps, multiple devices, or both, you'll have one provisioning profile for each combination displayed in Xcode (Figure 7-29).

Now that your provisioning profile is available in Xcode, you need to update the bundle identifier for your app. Select the appropriate provisioning profile in the Xcode organizer window and copy the app identifier (Figure 7-30).

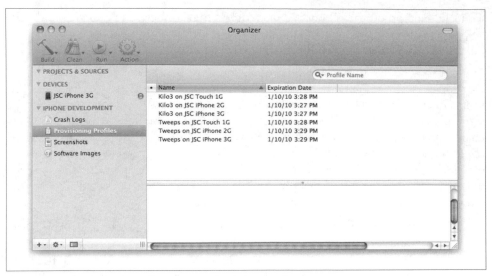

Figure 7-29. Multiple provisioning profiles loaded in Xcode

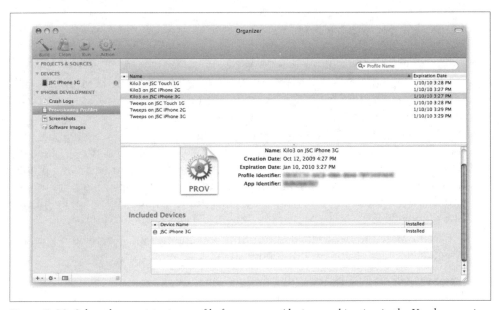

Figure 7-30. Select the provisioning profile for your app/device combination in the Xcode organizer window to locate your app identifier

Then, click PhoneGap→Config→Info.plist in the Groups & Files panel of the main Xcode window, and paste the app identifier into the bundle identifier field. If your app identifier ends with an asterisk, replace the asterisk with a reverse domain-name–style string such as `com.jonathanstark.kilo` (Figure 7-31).

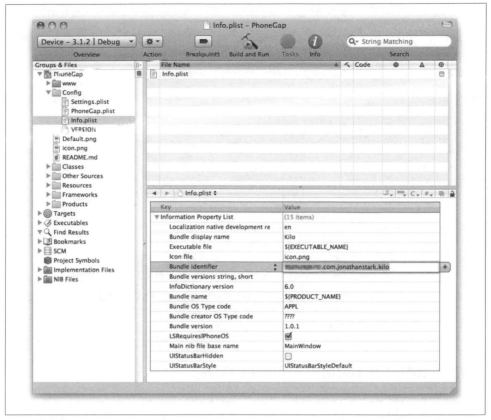

Figure 7-31. Paste your app identifier into the bundle identifier field, replacing the asterisk with a reverse domain-name–style string

Now, plug your iPhone into your computer and select the iPhone device option as your active SDK (Figure 7-32). Make sure to choose the iPhone device version that matches the version of iPhone OS you are running on your iPhone (the most recent is 3.1.2 as of this writing). Save the *Info.plist* file, clean the project (click Build→Clean), and click the Build and Run button. After about 20 seconds, the app should launch on your iPhone. The first time you launch it, you'll be prompted to allow the *codesign* application access to your keychain, and you'll also be prompted to install the provisioning profile on your iPhone. If you get any errors, restart Xcode and try again.

Now that the app is running on an actual iPhone, we can add some device-specific features.

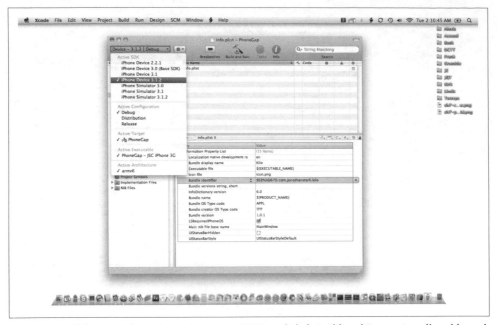

Figure 7-32. Select Device 3.1.2 as your active SDK, and click Build and Run to install and launch your app on your iPhone

Controlling the iPhone with JavaScript

The stage is now set for us to start enhancing our application with calls to the native device features. PhoneGap makes this possible by exposing certain functionality via JavaScript. This means that all you have to do to make the phone vibrate is add a bit of JavaScript to your code. For example:

```
navigator.notification.vibrate();
```

Pretty simple, right?

Beep, Vibrate, and Alert

PhoneGap makes beep, vibrate, and alert functions so simple that I'm going to lump them together into one example. Specifically, we'll set up the app to beep, vibrate, and display a custom alert when the user creates an entry that puts her over her daily calorie budget. To do this, add the following function to the end of *kilo.js*:

```
function checkBudget() {❶
    var currentDate = sessionStorage.currentDate;
    var dailyBudget = localStorage.budget;
    db.transaction(❷
        function(transaction) {
            transaction.executeSql(❸
```

```
                      'SELECT SUM(calories) AS currentTotal FROM entries WHERE date = ?;',❹
                      [currentDate], ❺
                      function (transaction, result) {❻
                          var currentTotal = result.rows.item(0).currentTotal;❼
                          if (currentTotal > dailyBudget) {❽
                              var overage = currentTotal - dailyBudget;❾
                              var message = 'You are '+overage
                              + ' calories over your daily budget.
                              + ' Better start jogging!',❿
                              try {⓫
                                  navigator.notification.beep();
                                  navigator.notification.vibrate();
                              } catch(e){
                                  // No equivalent in web app
                              }
                              try {⓬
                                  navigator.notification.alert(message,
                                      'Over Budget', 'Dang!');
                              } catch(e) {
                                  alert(message);
                              }
                          }
                      },
                      errorHandler⓭
              );
          }
      );
  }
```

Here's the blow-by-blow description:

❶ Open the checkBudget() function. Initialize the currentDate variable to the value stored in sessionStorage (i.e., the value entered by the user in the Settings panel), and the dailyBudget variable to the value stored in localStorage (i.e., the date tapped on the Dates panel).

❷ Start a database transaction in preparation for calculating the total calories for the current date.

❸ Run the executeSql() method of the transaction object.

Let's break down the four parameters of the executeSql() method:

❹ The first parameter is a prepared SQL statement that uses the SUM function to add up all the values in the calories column for the entries that match the current date.

❺ The second parameter is a single-value array that will replace the question mark in the prepared statement on the previous line.

❻ The third parameter is an anonymous function that will be called if the SQL query completes successfully (we'll look at this in detail momentarily).

And here is what's going on in the anonymous function that was passed in as the third parameter:

❼ It starts off by grabbing the current total from the first row of the result. Since we are just asking for the sum of a column, the database is only going to return one row (i.e., this query will always return one row). Remember that the records of the result set are accessed with the `item()` method of the rows property of the result object, and that the rows are 0 based (meaning that the first row is 0).

❽ Check to see if the current calorie total for the day is greater than the daily budget specified on the Settings panel. If so, the block that follows will be executed.

❾ Calculate how far the user is over her calorie budget.

❿ Compose a message to display to the user.

⓫ This is a `try/catch` block that attempts to call the `beep()` and `vibrate()` methods of the navigator notification object. These methods only exist in PhoneGap, so if the user is running the app in a browser, the methods will fail and execution will jump to the `catch` block. Since there is no browser-based equivalent to beep or vibrate, the `catch` block has been left empty.

The PhoneGap `beep()` method plays a *.wav* file when called. The file is named *beep.wav* and lives in the *iphone* directory (Figure 7-33). The default file sounds sort of like a cricket and is probably fine for most situations. If you'd prefer your own beep sound, just create a *.wav* file named *beep.wav* and replace the default file in the *iphone* directory.

⓬ This is a `try/catch` block that attempts to call the `alert()` method of the navigator notification object. This method only exists in PhoneGap, so if the user is running the app in a browser, the method will fail and execution will jump to the `catch` block. The browser-based equivalent to the PhoneGap alert is a standard JavaScript alert, which is called as a fallback.

There are a couple of differences between the PhoneGap alert and the native JavaScript alert. For example, the PhoneGap alert allows you to control the title and the button name (Figure 7-34); the JavaScript alert does not (Figure 7-35).

There is also a more subtle difference between the two alerts: the native JavaScript alert is modal and the PhoneGap alert is not. In other words, script execution will pause at the point at which you call a native alert, whereas execution will continue with the PhoneGap version. This may or may not be a big deal depending on the nature of your application, so keep this distinction in mind.

⓭ The fourth parameter is the name of the generic SQL error handler that will be called in the event of a SQL error.

With our `checkBudget()` function complete, we can now call it by adding a single line to the success callback of our `createEntry()` function:

```
function createEntry() {
    var date = sessionStorage.currentDate;
    var calories = $('#calories').val();
    var food = $('#food').val();
    db.transaction(
        function(transaction) {
            transaction.executeSql(
                'INSERT INTO entries (date, calories, food) VALUES (?, ?, ?),',
                [date, calories, food],
                function(){
                    refreshEntries();
                    checkBudget();
                    jQT.goBack();
                },
                errorHandler
            );
        }
    );
    return false;
}
```

After you've made these changes, save the *kilo.js* file, clean the project (Build→Clean),
and click Build and Run.

Figure 7-33. The PhoneGap beep() method plays the beep.wav file from the iphone directory

Figure 7-34. The PhoneGap alert allows you to specify the title and button label

Figure 7-35. A native JavaScript alert does not allow you to specify the title and button label

Geolocation

Let's update Kilo to save the location where entries are created. Once we have that information, we'll add a "Map Location" button that will open the built-in Maps application and drop a pin at the point where the entry was created.

The first step is to add latitude and longitude columns to the database to store the information. To do so, replace the CREATE TABLE statement in *kilo.js* with the following:

```
db.transaction(
    function(transaction) {
        transaction.executeSql(
            'CREATE TABLE IF NOT EXISTS entries ' +
            '   (id INTEGER NOT NULL PRIMARY KEY AUTOINCREMENT, ' +
            '    date DATE NOT NULL, food TEXT NOT NULL, ' +
            '    calories INTEGER NOT NULL, ' +
            '    longitude TEXT NOT NULL, latitude TEXT NOT NULL);'
        );
    }
);
```

Next, we'll rewrite the createEntry() function that we first saw in "Inserting Rows" on page 79 to use the geolocation feature of the phone to determine the current latitude and longitude. Replace the existing createEntry() function in *kilo.js* with this:

```
function createEntry() {❶
    try {❷
        navigator.geolocation.getCurrentPosition(❸
            function(position){❹
                var latitude = position.coords.latitude;❺
                var longitude = position.coords.longitude;
                insertEntry(latitude, longitude);❻
            },
            function(){❼
                insertEntry();❽
            }
        );
    } catch(e) {❾
        insertEntry();❿
    }
    return false;⓫
}
```

❶ Begin the createEntry() function.

❷ Open a try block, because the navigator.geolocation call will fail if this code is run outside of PhoneGap.

❸ Call the getCurrentPosition() function of the geolocation object and pass it two callback functions: one for success and one for errors.

❹ This is the beginning of the success callback. Notice that it accepts a single parameter (position).

❺ These two lines grab the latitude and longitude coordinates out of the position object.

❻ Pass the latitude and longitude coordinates into a function called insertEntry(), which we'll look at momentarily.

❼ This is the beginning of the error callback.

➑ Because we're in the error callback, this will only be called if geolocation failed (perhaps the user did not allow the application to access his location when prompted), so call the insertEntry() function without parameters.

➒ Begin the catch block.

➓ Because we're in the catch block, this means that the navigator.geolocation call failed, so call the insertEntry() function without parameters.

⓫ Return false to prevent the default navigation behavior of clicking the form's submit button.

Wondering where the SQL INSERT statement got to? Let's take a look at the insertEntry() function. This new function is what creates the entry in the database. Add the following to *kilo.js*:

```
function insertEntry(latitude, longitude) {❶
    var date = sessionStorage.currentDate;❷
    var calories = $('#calories').val();❸
    var food = $('#food').val();❹
    db.transaction(❺
        function(transaction) {❻
            transaction.executeSql(❼
                'INSERT INTO entries (date, calories, food, latitude, longitude) ' +
                    'VALUES (?, ?, ?, ?, ?);',❽
                [date, calories, food, latitude, longitude],❾
                function(){❿
                    refreshEntries();
                    checkBudget();
                    jQT.goBack();
                },
                errorHandler⓫
            );
        }
    );
}
```

❶ The beginning of the insertEntry() function, allowing for latitude and longitude values to be passed in. Although there is no way to explicitly mark a parameter as optional in JavaScript, these values will simply be undefined if they are not passed in.

❷ Get the currentDate out of sessionStorage. Remember that the value will be set when the user taps an item on the Dates panel to navigate to the Date panel. When he taps the + button to reveal the New Entry panel, this value will still be set to the currently selected Date panel item.

❸ Get the calories value out of the createEntry form.

❹ Get the food value out of the createEntry form.

❺ Begin a database transaction.

❻ Pass a callback function into the transaction, with the transaction object as its sole parameter.

❼ Call the `executeSql()` method of the transaction object.

❽ Define the SQL prepared statement with question marks as data placeholders.

❾ Pass an array of values for the placeholders. If `latitude` and `longitude` were not passed into the `insertEntry()` function, they will be undefined.

❿ Define the success callback function.

⓫ Define the error callback function.

In order to confirm that Kilo is actually saving these location values, we'll want to display them somewhere in the interface. Let's add an Inspect Entry panel to display the stored values. We'll include a Map Location button on the panel that will display where the entry was created. Add the following to *index.html*, right before the closing body tag (`</body>`):

```
<div id="inspectEntry">
    <div class="toolbar">
        <h1>Inspect Entry</h1>
        <a class="button cancel" href="#">Cancel</a>
    </div>
    <form method="post">
        <ul class="rounded">
            <li><input type="text" placeholder="Food" name="food" value="" /></li>
            <li><input type="tel" placeholder="Calories" name="calories"
                value="" /></li>❶
            <li><input type="submit" value="Save Changes" /></li>
        </ul>
        <ul class="rounded">
            <li><input type="text" name="latitude" value="" /></li>❷
            <li><input type="text" name="longitude" value="" /></li>
            <li><p class="whiteButton" id="mapLocation">Map Location</p></li>❸
        </ul>
    </form>
</div>
```

This should look very similar to the New Entry panel that we first saw in Example 4-5, so I'll just call out a couple of things.

❶ The input type has been set to `tel` to call the telephone keyboard when the cursor is placed in the field. This is a bit of a hack, but I think it's worth it because that keyboard is much more appropriate for this field.

❷ The `latitude` and `longitude` fields are editable and contained within the form, which means that the user is able to edit them. This probably would not make sense in the final application, but it makes it a lot easier to test during development because you can enter location values manually to test the mapping button.

❸ This Map Location button won't do anything when clicked at this point; we'll add a click handler to it momentarily.

Now we need to give the user a way to navigate to this Inspect Entry panel, so we'll modify the behavior of the Date panel such that when the user taps an entry in the list, the Inspect Entry panel will slide up from the bottom of the screen.

The first step is to wire up the click event handler (which we'll create next), and also to modify the way clicks on the Delete button are processed. Add the three highlighted changes below to the refreshEntries() function in *kilo.js*:

```
function refreshEntries() {
    var currentDate = sessionStorage.currentDate;
    $('#date h1').text(currentDate);
    $('#date ul li:gt(0)').remove();
    db.transaction(
        function(transaction) {
            transaction.executeSql(
                'SELECT * FROM entries WHERE date = ? ORDER BY food;',
                [currentDate],
                function (transaction, result) {
                    for (var i=0; i < result.rows.length; i++) {
                        var row = result.rows.item(i);
                        var newEntryRow = $('#entryTemplate').clone();
                        newEntryRow.removeAttr('id');
                        newEntryRow.removeAttr('style');
                        newEntryRow.data('entryId', row.id);
                        newEntryRow.appendTo('#date ul');
                        newEntryRow.find('.label').text(row.food);
                        newEntryRow.find('.calories').text(row.calories);
                        newEntryRow.find('.delete').click(function(e){❶
                            var clickedEntry = $(this).parent();
                            var clickedEntryId = clickedEntry.data('entryId');
                            deleteEntryById(clickedEntryId);
                            clickedEntry.slideUp();
                            e.stopPropagation();❷
                        });
                        newEntryRow.click(entryClickHandler);❸
                    }
                },
                errorHandler
            );
        }
    );
}
```

❶ Note that we have to add the e parameter (the event) to the function call in order to have access to the stopPropagation() method of the event, used shortly. If we didn't add the e parameter, e.stopPropagation() would be undefined.

❷ The e.stopPropagation(); added to the Delete button click handler tells the browser not to let the click event bubble up the DOM (Document Object Model) to parent elements. This is important because we've now added a click handler to the row itself, and the entry row is the parent of the Delete button. If we didn't call stopPropagation(), both the Delete button handler and the entryClickHandler would fire when the user tapped the Delete button.

❸ The `newEntryRow.click(entryClickHandler);` tells the browser to call the `entryClickHandler` function when the entry is tapped.

Now let's add the `entryClickHandler()` function to *kilo.js*:

```
function entryClickHandler(e){
    sessionStorage.entryId = $(this).data('entryId');❶
    db.transaction(❷
        function(transaction) {❸
            transaction.executeSql(❹
                'SELECT * FROM entries WHERE id = ?;', ❺
                [sessionStorage.entryId], ❻
                function (transaction, result) {❼
                    var row = result.rows.item(0);❽
                    var food = row.food;❾
                    var calories = row.calories;
                    var latitude = row.latitude;
                    var longitude = row.longitude;
                    $('#inspectEntry input[name="food"]').val(food);❿
                    $('#inspectEntry input[name="calories"]').val(calories);
                    $('#inspectEntry input[name="latitude"]').val(latitude);
                    $('#inspectEntry input[name="longitude"]').val(longitude);
                    $('#mapLocation').click(function(){⓫
                        window.location = 'http://maps.google.com/maps?z=15&q='+
                            food+'@'+latitude+','+longitude;
                    });
                    jQT.goTo('#inspectEntry', 'slideup');⓬
                },
                errorHandler⓭
            );
        }
    );
}
```

❶ Get the `entryId` from the entry that the user tapped and store it in session storage.

❷ Begin a database transaction.

❸ Pass a callback function into the transaction, with the transaction object as its sole parameter.

❹ Call the `executeSql()` method of the transaction object

❺ Define the SQL prepared statement with a question mark as data placeholder.

❻ Pass a single-element array for the placeholder.

❼ Begin the success callback function.

❽ Get the first (and only, since we're just querying for one entry) row of the result.

❾ Set some variables based on the values from the row.

❿ Set values of the form fields based on the variables.

⓫ Attach a click handler to the `#mapLocation` button. The function sets the window location to a standard Google Maps URL. If the Maps application is available, it will launch. Otherwise, the URL will load in a browser. The z value sets the initial zoom level; the string before the @ symbol will be used as the label for the pin that is dropped at the location. Note that the latitude and longitude values must appear in the order shown here, separated by a comma.

⓬ Call the goTo() method of the jQTouch object to make the Inspect Entry panel slide up into view.

⓭ Define the error callback function.

Before you try running the app, be sure to delete it from the phone (or the simulator). That's because the database won't be created if it already exists, and an easy way to remove the database is to remove the app. To remove the app, tap and hold on its home screen icon until the icons start wobbling, then click the X to remove it. Press the home button to stop the wobbling. Then, clean the project (Build→Clean) and click "Build and Run" to try it out.

Accelerometer

Next, let's set up Kilo to duplicate the last entry in the list by shaking the phone. Add the following function to the end of *kilo.js*:

```
function dupeEntryById(entryId) {
    if (entryId == undefined) {❶
        alert('You have to have at least one entry in the list to shake a dupe.');
    } else {
        db.transaction(❷
            function(transaction) {
                transaction.executeSql(
                    ' INSERT INTO entries (date, food, calories, latitude, longitude)'
                    + ' SELECT date, food, calories, latitude, longitude'❸
                    + ' FROM entries WHERE id = ?;',
                    [entryId], ❹
                    function() {❺
                        refreshEntries();
                    },
                    errorHandler❻
                );
            }
        );
    }
}
```

❶ This line makes sure that an entryId was passed to the function. If not, the user is notified.

❷ Begin the usual database transaction steps.

❸ Define an INSERT statement that copies the values from the specified entryId. This is a type of query you haven't seen before. Instead of using a list of values for the INSERT, this takes the values from a SELECT query for the specified entryId.

❹ Pass the `entryId` into the prepared statement, replacing the `?` in the SELECT query with the value of the `entryId`.

❺ On success, call `refreshEntries()`, which will display the newly copied entry.

❻ On error, call the standard SQL error handler.

Now we need to tell the application when to start and stop watching the accelerometer. We'll set it up to start watching when the Date panel finishes sliding into view, and to stop when it starts sliding out. To do this, we just need to add the following lines to the document ready function in *kilo.js*:

```
$('#date').bind('pageAnimationEnd', function(e, info){❶
    if (info.direction == 'in') {❷
        startWatchingShake();
    }
});
$('#date').bind('pageAnimationStart', function(e, info){❸
    if (info.direction == 'out') {❹
        stopWatchingShake();
    }
});
```

❶ Bind an anonymous handler to the `pageAnimationEnd` event of the `#date` panel. Pass the event and the additional info in as parameters.

❷ Check to see if the `direction` property of the info object equals `in`. If it does, call the `startWatchingShake()` function, which we'll look at shortly.

❸ Bind an anonymous handler to the `pageAnimationBegin` event of the `#date` panel. Pass the event and the additional info in as parameters.

❹ Check to see if the `direction` property of the info object equals `out`. If it does, call the `stopWatchingShake()` function, which we'll look at shortly.

Technically, we could have bound to just one of the page animation events, like so:

```
$('#date').bind('pageAnimationEnd', function(e, info){
    if (info.direction == 'in') {
        startWatchingShake();
    } else {
        stopWatchingShake();
    }
});
```

The reason I didn't do this is that `stopWatchingShake()` would not get called until after the page animation was complete. Therefore, the accelerometer would be actively watched during the page transition, which can sometimes result in choppy animation.

All that's left for us to do is write the `startWatchingShake()` and `stopWatchingShake()` functions. Add the following functions to the end of *kilo.js*:

```
function startWatchingShake() {❶
    var success = function(coords){❷
        var max = 2;❸
        if (Math.abs(coords.x) > max
        || Math.abs(coords.y) > max
        || Math.abs(coords.z) > max) {❹
            var entryId = $('#date ul li:last').data('entryId');❺
            dupeEntryById(entryId);❻
        }
    };
    var error = function(){};❼
    var options = {};❽
    options.frequency = 100;❾
    sessionStorage.watchId = navigator.accelerometer.watchAcceleration(success,
        error, options);❿
}
function stopWatchingShake() {⓫
    navigator.accelerometer.clearWatch(sessionStorage.watchId);⓬
}
```

❶ Begin the `startWatchingShake()` function. This function will be called when the `#date` panel finishes animating into view.

❷ Begin defining the success handler. Note that it accepts a coordinates object as its sole parameter.

❸ Define the threshold for the shake. The higher the number, the harder the user will have to shake.

❹ Check to see if any of the coordinates has exceeded the threshold.

❺ Get the `entryId` of the last entry on the `#date` panel.

❻ Call the `dupeEntryById()` function.

❼ Define an empty error handler.

❽ Define an `options` object to pass into the `watchAcceleration()` method of the accelerometer object.

❾ The `frequency` property of the `options` object allows you to specify (in milliseconds) how often you want your app to check the accelerometer.

❿ Call the `watchAcceleration()` method of the `accelerometer` object, passing in the success handler, the error handler, and the `options` object as parameters. Store the result in `sessionStorage.watchId`, which we'll need for the `stopWatchingShake()` function.

⓫ Begin the `stopWatchingShake()` function. This function will be called when the `#date` panel starts animating out of view.

⓬ Call the `clearWatch()` method of the `accelerometer` object, passing it the `watchId` from session storage.

And with that, we are ready to test. Save all your files, clean all targets, and build and run Kilo on your device. Navigate to the Date panel, add an entry if none exists, and shake the phone. You should see the page reload with an additional entry. Unfortunately, you'll probably also see an Undo confirmation dialog (Figure 7-36). To disable the undo manager so we can watch the accelerometer without being interrupted, we need to add a setting to *Info.plist*. Follow the steps described in "Adding Settings to Info.plist" on page 126 to add a setting for UIApplicationSupportsShakeToEdit, and set it to false (Figure 7-37).

Figure 7-36. We need to deactivate the undo manager to watch the accelerometer in peace

Key	Value
▼ Information Property List	(17 items)
Localization native development re	en
Bundle display name	Kilo
Executable file	${EXECUTABLE_NAME}
Icon file	icon.png
Bundle identifier	9SZN26J67D.com.jonathanstark.kilo
InfoDictionary version	6.0
Bundle name	${PRODUCT_NAME}
Bundle OS Type code	APPL
Bundle creator OS Type code	????
Bundle version	1.0.1
LSRequiresIPhoneOS	☑
Main nib file base name	
UIStatusBarHidden	☐
UIStatusBarStyle	UIStatusBarStyleBlackOpaque
Bundle versions string, short	
UIPrerenderedIcon	☑
UIApplicationSupportsShakeToEdit	☐

Figure 7-37. Add the UIApplicationSupportsShakeToEdit setting to Info.plist and leave it unchecked to disable "shake to undo" in your app

What You've Learned

In this chapter, you've learned how to load your web app into PhoneGap, how to install your app on your iPhone, and how to access five device features that are unavailable to browser-based web apps (beep, alert, vibrate, geolocation, and accelerometer).

In the next chapter, you'll learn how to package your app as an executable and submit it to the iTunes App Store.

Submitting Your App to iTunes

Finally, the moment you've been waiting for: submitting your completed app to iTunes. There are several steps to the process, and you'll want to have all your ducks in a row before you get started. At a minimum, you'll need the following to complete the App Store submission process:

- A plain-text description for the application (4,000 characters max).
- A URL where people can learn more about your app.
- A support URL and email address so people can contact you with issues pertaining to your app.
- If your app requires a login, full access credentials for a demo account so reviewers can test your app.
- A 512 × 512 pixel icon.
- A 320 × 480 pixel screenshot of your app.
- A distribution provisioning profile for the app.
- A zipped version of the application binary.

Everything you need for submission is fairly straightforward except for the last two items: the distribution profile for the app, and the application binary. We'll cover those in detail in the following sections.

 Wherever I refer to Kilo in this chapter, please substitute the name you are going to use for your app.

Creating an iPhone Distribution Provisioning Profile

In Chapter 7, you created a *development* provisioning profile that allowed you to test your app on an actual iPhone. Now, you need to create a *distribution* provisioning profile in order to submit the app to iTunes.

1. Navigate to the iPhone developer site (*http://developer.apple.com/iphone/*) and log in.

2. Click iPhone Developer Program Portal in the right sidebar.

3. Click on Provisioning in the left sidebar.

4. Click on the Distribution tab.

5. Click the New Profile button.

6. Choose App Store as your distribution method.

7. Enter a profile name (e.g., Kilo Distribution Provisioning Profile).

8. If you have not created a distribution certificate, you should do so before proceeding. If you see a link on this page labeled "Please create a Distribution Certificate," click it and carefully follow the instructions. You'll be making a couple of trips into the Keychain Access application (located in */Applications/Utilities*) to create *certificate signing requests* and to install signed certificates that you download from the portal into your own keychain.

9. Select the appropriate App ID (Figure 8-1).

10. Click the Submit button (you'll be returned to the Distribution Provisioning Profile list view).

11. Refresh the page until the Download button appears (Figure 8-2).

12. Click the Download button to save the profile to your local download directory (usually the *Downloads* folder in your Home folder).

13. Drag the downloaded profile onto the Xcode icon in the dock.

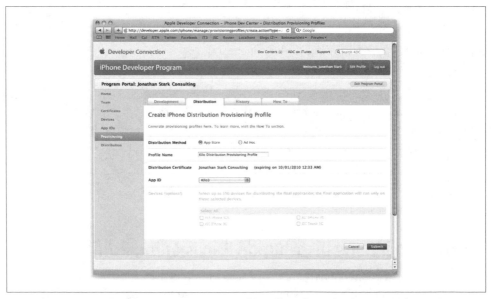

Figure 8-1. Create a distribution provisioning profile in the iPhone developer portal

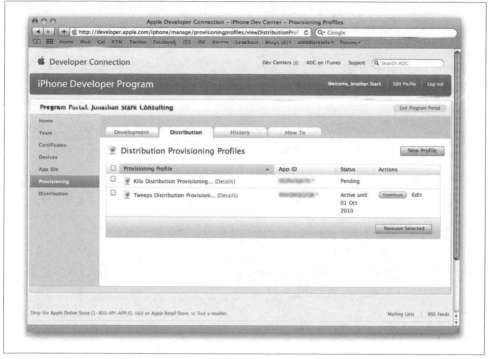

Figure 8-2. Refresh the distribution profile list until the Download button appears

Installing the iPhone Distribution Provisioning Profile

Now that the profile is in Xcode, you need to configure the project to use it.

1. Open Kilo in Xcode if it's not already open.
2. Select Edit Project Settings from the Project menu (the project settings window will appear).
3. Click the Build tab if it's not already active.
4. Select Distribution from the Configuration pop up.
5. Select "Settings Defined at This Level" from the Show pop up.
6. Locate Code Signing→Code Signing Identity→Any iPhone OS Device in the main area of the window.
7. Click the pop-up list to the right of Any iPhone OS Device to display a list of profile options (Figure 8-3).
8. Locate your distribution provisioning profile in the list and select the distribution identity directly beneath it (Figure 8-4).
9. Close the Project Info window.

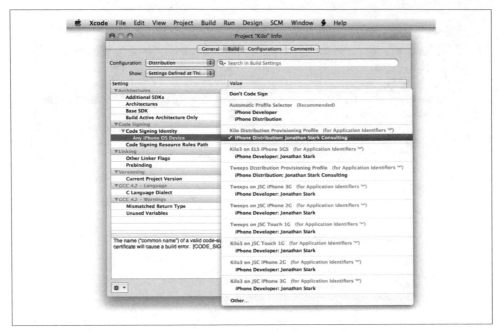

Figure 8-3. Click the pop-up list next to Any iPhone OS Device

Figure 8-4. The distribution identity is located directly beneath the distribution profile

Renaming the Project

Before you submit your app, you need to rename it from PhoneGap to Kilo. To do so:

1. Open the project in Xcode.
2. Select Rename from the Project menu (Figure 8-5).
3. Type Kilo in the "Rename project to" field (Figure 8-6).
4. You can leave "Take Snapshot before renaming" checked if you want to save the state of the project prior to making the change, but it will significantly increase the amount of time it takes to process the request.
5. Click the Rename button.

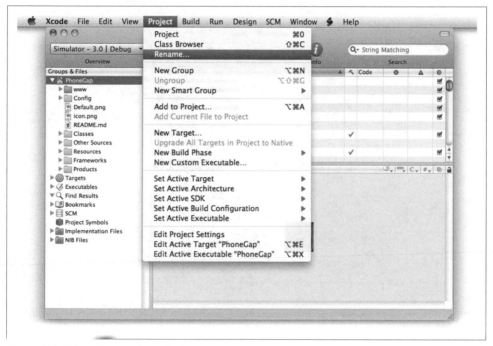

Figure 8-5. Select Rename from the Project menu

You will see a series of green circles with white checkmarks in them that indicate that the changes have taken effect (Figure 8-7).

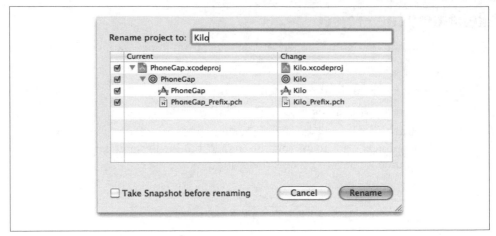

Figure 8-6. Type Kilo in the "Rename project to" field

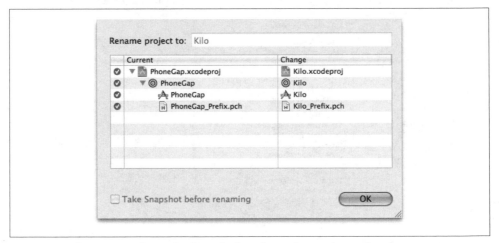

Figure 8-7. The green circles with white checkmarks in them indicate that the renaming process succeeded

Prepare the Application Binary

Next, we need to build the application executable and prepare it to be uploaded.

1. Select iPhone Device - 3.1.2 (or the current version of the iPhone OS) from the Active SDK pop up, then select it again and pick Distribution. This should set the target to something like "Device - 3.1.2 | Distribution."

2. Select Clean All Targets from the Build menu.

3. Select Build from the Build menu. You may be prompted to allow the application *codesign* to access your keychain. Allow it to do this so it can sign the app.

4. Make sure that you didn't get any errors.

5. Reveal the app in the Finder (Figure 8-8).

6. Compress the app into a ZIP archive (Figure 8-9).

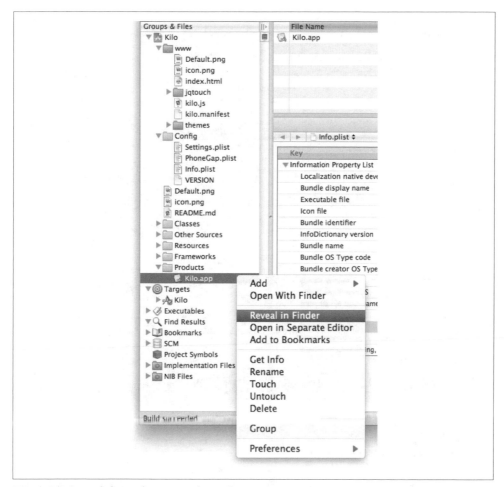

Figure 8-8. Reveal the application in the Finder

Submit Your App

Now that you have everything you need:

1. Log in to iTunes Connect (*https://itunesconnect.apple.com/*).

2. Click on Manage Your Applications.

3. Click on the Add New Application button.

4. Follow the onscreen instructions to proceed with the submission process.

5. Hurry up and wait.

If all goes well, you should see your app listed as In Review (Figure 8-10).

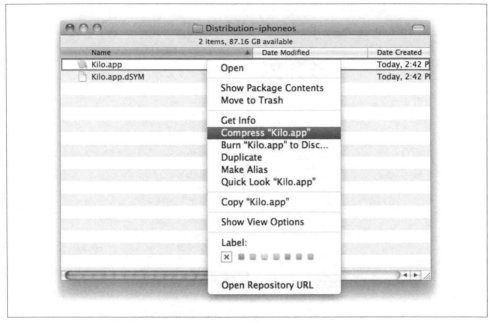

Figure 8-9. The application must be compressed as a ZIP archive to be uploaded

Figure 8-10. The uploaded app will appear in your list with a status of In Review

While You Wait

Congratulations! You've officially submitted your first app to the iTunes App Store! Now what? You'll probably have to wait a week or two to hear back from Apple. Here are some things you can do in the meantime to keep yourself busy:

- Set up a nice-looking web page for your app that is located at the URL that you submitted to Apple. Be sure to include the following elements:
  - A video of your app in action. Loren Brichter (*http://twitter.com/atebits*) has posted a great tutorial on making beautiful iPhone screencasts at *http://blog .atebits.com/2009/03/not-your-average-iphone-screencast/*.
  - A brief description of your app. Just a paragraph or two and 5–10 bullet points.
  - An iTunes link to purchase your app.
  - A few testimonials, with a link to more if you have them.
  - A support email address. You could opt to set up a support forum instead, but you'll learn more about your customers via email.
- Send personal email messages to bloggers who you think would be interested in your app. Target blogs that are relevant to the market for your app, and blogs that are about the iPhone in general.
- Clean out your inbox. You'll probably get about 5–20 email messages per 100 sales, so if your app is popular, you're going to be getting a lot of email. Start with a clean slate!
- Start working on your first upgrade. The more popular apps seem to upgrade about twice a month, which causes a steady buzz and lots of customer goodwill.

Further Reading

If you find yourself in a jam, here are some helpful resources:

- jQTouch Issue Tracker: *http://code.google.com/p/jqtouch/issues/list*
- jQTouch on Twitter: *http://twitter.com/jqtouch*
- jQTouch Wiki: *http://code.google.com/p/jqtouch/w/list*
- PhoneGap Google Group: *http://groups.google.com/group/phonegap*
- PhoneGap on Twitter: *http://twitter.com/phonegap*
- PhoneGap Wiki: *http://phonegap.pbworks.com/*
- jQuery Documentation: *http://docs.jquery.com/*
- W3C Spec for Offline Applications: *http://dev.w3.org/html5/spec/Overview.html #offline*

Index

We'd like to hear your suggestions for improving our indexes. Send email to *index@oreilly.com*.

X

About the Author

Jonathan Stark is a mobile and web application consultant who the *Wall Street Journal* has called an expert on publishing desktop data to the Web. He has written two books on web application programming, is a tech editor for *php|architect* and *Advisor* magazines, and has been quoted in the media on Internet and mobile lifestyle trends.

Colophon

The animal on the cover of *Building iPhone Apps with HTML, CSS, and JavaScript* is a bluebird (genus *Sialia*, family *Turdidae*). Although they are predominantly blue in color, bluebirds can have vivid shades of red dispersed throughout their plumage. Unlike other species of birds, no discernible difference exists in the color patterns of male and female bluebirds.

The birds are territorial by nature and favor open grasslands with scattered trees. Males will identify nest sites among the trees and will try to attract prospective mates by singing, flapping their wings, and then depositing some material within the cavities of those trees. If a female accepts the male's entreaties and one of the nesting sites, she alone will build the nest for the home.

Bluebirds are unique to North America, and bird lovers often attract them to their backyards with feeders full of darkling beetles and mealworms. Bluebirds are also fond of eating raisins soaked in water and bathing in heated birdbaths.

The bird is popularly thought of as a symbol of optimism, although occasionally this symbolism goes into shadowier terrain.

Some dream interpreters say the image of a dead bluebird represents disillusionment, a loss of innocence, and a transition from a younger, more naïve self to a wiser one, while the image of a live bluebird represents spiritual joy and contentedness, or a longing for such a state. Judy Garland's character Dorothy in *The Wizard of Oz* perhaps exemplifies this longing when she sings about happy little bluebirds in the song "Somewhere over the Rainbow."

The cover image is from *Johnson's Natural History*. The cover font is Adobe ITC Garamond. The text font is Linotype Birka; the heading font is Adobe Myriad Condensed; and the code font is LucasFont's TheSansMonoCondensed.

Get even more for your money.

Join the O'Reilly Community, and register the O'Reilly books you own. It's free, and you'll get:

- 40% upgrade offer on O'Reilly books
- Membership discounts on books and events
- Free lifetime updates to electronic formats of books
- Multiple ebook formats, DRM FREE
- Participation in the O'Reilly community
- Newsletters
- Account management
- 100% Satisfaction Guarantee

Signing up is easy:

1. **Go to: oreilly.com/go/register**
2. **Create an O'Reilly login.**
3. **Provide your address.**
4. **Register your books.**

Note: English-language books only

To order books online:

oreilly.com/order_new

For questions about products or an order:

orders@oreilly.com

To sign up to get topic-specific email announcements and/or news about upcoming books, conferences, special offers, and new technologies:

elists@oreilly.com

For technical questions about book content:

booktech@oreilly.com

To submit new book proposals to our editors:

proposals@oreilly.com

Many O'Reilly books are available in PDF and several ebook formats. For more information:

oreilly.com/ebooks

O'REILLY®

Spreading the knowledge of innovators   www.oreilly.com